West Penwith at the Time of Charles II

By the

Penwith Local History Group 1998

TWO-HEARTH COTTAGE WITH ROPED THATCH. BASED UPON INFORMATION COLLECTED BY ERIC BERRY.

Editor- Helen Beaufort-Murphy
With illustrations by S. J. Haxton

Published by the Penwith Local History Group

Printed by the St. Ives Printing and Publishing Company

ISBN 0 952 4744 1 7

Copyright © is vested in the authors who take responsibility for the content of their articles. They may be contacted through the Morrab Library, Penzance.

No part of this publication may be reproduced, stored in a retrieval system, or transmitted in any form or by any means, electronic, mechanical, photocopying, recording or otherwise without the prior permission of the copyright holders.

We particularly wish to thank the staff of the Cornwall Record Office (CRO), the Royal Institution of Cornwall (RIC), the Cornish Studies Library (CSL) and the Cornwall Mobile Library Service.

Our thanks also go to June Palmer for help with pre-publication sales, Audrey Pool for comments on continuity, Dawn Walker and Elsa Clee for typing, Justin Brooke for mining references, Lesley Lowden of the Morrab Library, our printers for advice, and all our families and friends who have worked so hard both physically and mentally in their support of us.

Much of the work in this book is based on The Cornwall Hearth Tax for 1664 which is in the Public Record Office (PRO) reference number E 179/244/44.

A speculative sketch of a cottage at Bosigran – one hearth with mullioned window on Rt. hand side (based on survey by Eric Berry)

Spelling was not standardised in the 17th century, particularly with surnames, and allowances should be made for this. Words often finished with a flourish which looked like 'e'. The handwriting can be very difficult to decipher, and impossible where time has taken its toll. In quoting from these documents some authors have kept to the original and some have modernised their extracts.

The old currency is used, except where stated, and given thus - £ s d. There were twelve pence (d) to the shilling (s) and twenty shillings to the pound (£).
A pound weight is 16 ounces or 450 grammes.

CONTENTS:

	Introduction	Jean Nankervis	5
	Prologue	Tom Arkell	6
I	Finding Out About the People who lived in West Penwith	Tom Arkell	7
II	Some One-Hearth Homes in West Penwith	Iris Green	11
III	The Parson's Evidence	Veronica Chesher	17
IV	Household Goods from West Penwith	Tom Arkell	22
V	Zennor at the Time of the Hearth Tax	Jean Nankervis	27
VI	West Penwith Sheep	Helen Beaufort-Murphy	35
	Coloured Plates (1–8)		40
VII	The Merchants of Penzance	Margaret E. Perry	49
VIII	Families and Neighbours in Penzance	Elsa Clee	55
IX	Richard Angwin of St. Just	Carlene Harry	59
X	The Quakers at Sennen	Gillian Green	64
XI	Francis Paynter and his Family	J. M. Hosking	69
	Surname Index		74
	Glossary		76

PENDEEN MANOR

Notes from the illustrator

The chapters in this volume are individual items based on considerable research and the artwork is an attempt to complement the academic composition. Whilst some of it is representational, I have researched its accuracy, and gained a great deal of enjoyment in the process. Many of the small sketches are of domestic items or scenes referred to in the text such as the 'book with two silver clasps' owned by Master Paynter of Boskenna. For this I made enquiries of a specialist bookbinder and restorer, Hilaria Honess, who described the type of silver clasp used at that date.

The illustration of the ship approaching Penzance is the size and type of vessel which plied a trade in these waters, although the purist will note that there is far too little rigging and will need to forgive that artistic license. From the various contemporary illustrations and some eighteenth century engravings I studied, I hope I have made a fair representation of the harbour and headland area. The illustration of St. Mary's Chapel was drawn by J.S.Prout in a 19th Century publication by J. Vibert. The chapel was demolished in 1832.

It was proposed that an illustration for the cover of the book should echo the work of the seventeenth century artist Schellinks, who portrayed figures viewing Mount's Bay from Long Rock. Thus, my figures overlooking Logan Rock suggest William Schellinks and his young companion Jaques Thierry.

Finally, my thanks to the many individuals who gave help and advised or simply came along on my field-trips to keep me company and to my family who put up with the disruption my artwork creates.

Steph Haxton

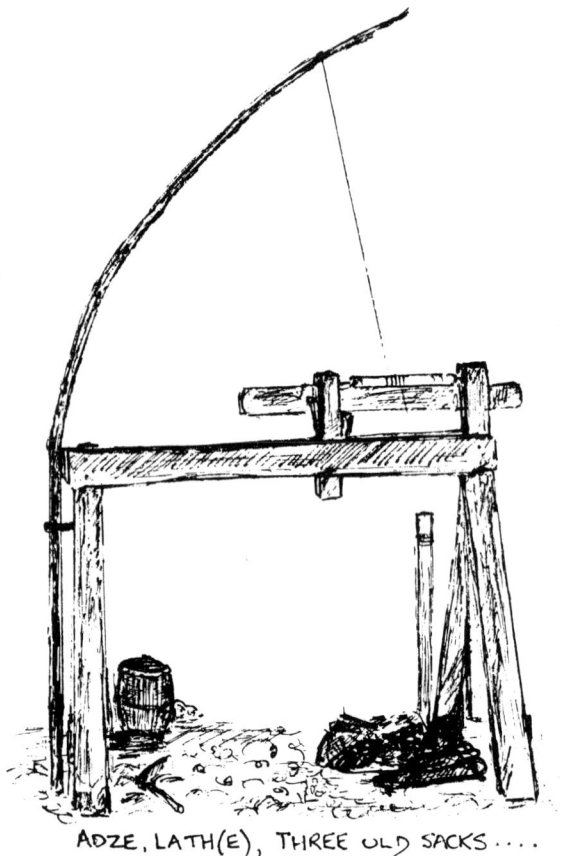

ADZE, LATH(E), THREE OLD SACKS....

A CAULDRON COOKING VARIOUS PARTS OF A MEAL - A 'JUGGED' CHICKEN WITH LID OF JAR SEALED WITH PASTRY, A NET OF VEGETABLES AND A BOILED PUDDING.

INTRODUCTION

'West Penwith at the Time of Charles II' began with a study of the Hearth Tax Returns for 1664 with members of the group choosing their favourite parishes. Wanting to know more than just the names of those on the list and how many hearths they had, members then researched specific subjects in greater depth. Using primary sources they unearthed fascinating facts about life at the end of the 17th century. Although Charles II reigned from 1660-'85 some of the the authors have written about events before and after this period.

Iris Green concentrated on the One-hearth house but what counted as a 'hearth' for taxation purposes? Not all fireplaces were enclosed with a chimney, an open hearth in the middle of a room was also chargeable. Veronica Chesher analysed terriers and describes the parsonages with their sparr thatched houses and the barns roofed with roped straw thatch. Jean Nankervis wanted to find out who lived where in Zennor and what farming was like. Elsa Clee, who lives in Towednack, found signs of conflict at those times between relations and neighbours, and Gillian Green studied the Quakers. Helen Beaufort-Murphy, having worked with farmers in Peru, Argentina, Chile, Uraguay and Bolivia, wrote about Penwith sheep and their bi-products. Tom Arkell is interested in statistics and made charts of who had what furniture and its value. Carlene Harry was intrigued by Richard Angwin of St. Just and Jim Hosking has a good story to tell about the Paynters from his forthcoming book. For the reader interested in family history Margaret Perry's research on Penzance merchants uncovered a seating plan for 220 named people for St. Mary's Chapel dated 1674 and there are a further 200 names in the surname index at the end of this book.

SHEPHERD AND SHEEP

We hope this book gives some unusual glimpses of the people of West Penwith and how they lived at the time of the Hearth Taxes.

PROLOGUE   A TOURIST'S VISIT TO LAND'S END IN 1662

TOM ARKELL

On Friday 1st August 1662 two Dutchmen rode out of Plymouth on horseback to visit Cornwall. One was the fourteen year old son of a very rich merchant ship owner, Jaques Thierry, who made huge profits from the notorious triangular Atlantic trade, selling slaves from West Africa to the English plantations in Barbados before taking their sugar back to London or Amsterdam. His son, also called Jaques, was now in the middle of a four year Grand Tour of Western Europe that included meeting many of his father's business contacts. His companion, or tutor, was William Shellinks, an accomplished topographical artist in his late thirties, who kept a detailed diary of their travels.

Their first three nights in Cornwall were spent at Fowey, before the two travellers moved on to Truro and then Falmouth. For the western-most part of their journey they were accompanied by one of their contacts, George Veale, who escorted them on Wednesday 6th to Penzance. There, `we stayed at the White Horse at Richard Veale's, vintner, the father of our travel companion, and were well provided for and had good accommodation'.

Next day, `we were prevented by rain from going to Land's End, so we looked at the market. As it was market day for fish and assorted goods, a lot of country people were at the market, everyone, men and women, young and old, puffing tobacco, which is here so common that the young get it in the morning instead of breakfast, and almost prefer it to bread. We went to see the market house and the harbour, which lies towards the west in Mount's Bay.'* That afternoon they visited St. Michael's Mount, where its owner, `Mr. John St. Aubyn, came to us, and welcomed us with great politeness, took us back to the hall and said he was greatly obliged and indebted to Mr Jaques Theirry and a thousand more such complements, and treated us there to small beer, etc.'* The tide was coming in fast as they left and so `we had to hurry if we wanted to go over on foot, and still had to wade through the water in boots, and Mr. Veale had to have himself carried over by a fisherman. After we had refreshed ourselves we rode back again to Penzance.'

The following morning they set out from Penzance at 8 o'clock to ride to Land's End, passing Newlyn `low down by the sea,' St. Buryan, St., Levan and Sennen. `We saw there many animals grazing at the outermost end of the land, where the land is very narrow. We rode on our horses as far as the steeply descending ground allowed.... To this uttermost westerly region mainly Quakers and such folk, also supposedly many witches and sorcerers.'* Next day, the 9th, St. Aubyn appeared at their lodgings in Marazion, where `he paid for a pint or two of wine, which we drank with him for friendship's sake, and so we took our leave, he strongly charging me to express his obedient affection to Mr. Jaques Thierry and to urge him to promote the affairs, and more of that kind. From there we rode to Helston, a nice market town, where it was market day. We ate our midday meal there, and Mr. G. Veale took his leave from us, we had in him a cheerful travel companion, who had kept us company all the way from Truro to here.'* Their visit to Cornwall lasted exactly a fortnight.

These selections from the diary of Shellinks give tantalising glimpses of West Penwith over three hundred years ago. Inevitably, they leave us wishing that he had stayed longer, found the road through St. Just and Zennor to St. Ives and described more of what he had seen. Because St. Michael's Mount fascinated him so much, he drew it five times, but nowhere else west of Falmouth, not even Land's End. And yet, this account of the visit provides us with a vivid introduction to West Penwith at the time of Charles II.

Source: M. Exwood and H.L. Lehmann (eds). ` The Journal of William Shellinks' Travel in England 1661-1663', Camden Fifth Series, Vol I, Royal Historical Society (1993), pp115-128.

I FINDING OUT ABOUT THE PEOPLE WHO LIVED IN WEST PENWITH

TOM ARKELL

The Hearth Tax

While Schellinks and young Jaques toured Cornwall in August 1662, the petty constables in every parish were busy preparing for a new tax. It was levied for the first time on 29th September (Michaelmas), when most householders paid a shilling for every hearth or fireplace in their house. Before this the names of those liable to pay were written down together with the number of their hearths. If the house was empty, they recorded the landlord's name.

Penwith's assessment list for Michaelmas 1662 has not survived, but the one for Michaelmas 1664 [1] has. It is especially interesting because it copied the first list, recorded most changes that had happened in the intervening two years and corrected some mistakes and omissions. Because very few poorer households exempt from paying the hearth tax were included, this list is not a complete record of all the householders who lived in West Penwith immediately after Charles II was restored, but it does name about two-thirds of them. Altogether 722 dwellings are listed for Penzance and the eleven most westerly parishes in Penwith which we have studied. They were distributed as follows:

Parish	Total households	1	2	3-5	6-9
Gulval	71	46	17	5	3
Madron	57	33	15	9	-
Penzance	103	44	25	29	5
Morvah	19	13	4	1	1
Paul	90	57	20	11	2
Sancreed	43	23	14	6	-
Sennen	21	17	2	2	-
St Buryan	95	59	24	11	2
St Just	118	72	30	13	3
St Levan	22	19	2	1	-
Towednack	34	23	10	1	-
Zennor	49	36	11	2	-
West Penwith	722	442	174	91	15

An early 17th century sword

Seventy-one of these 722 households were listed solely in 1664 and a mere 23 were recorded as being exempt from paying the tax (with 17 of these in St Just, St Buryan and Sancreed). All the 23 exempt had paid the hearth tax two years earlier and changed their status. Evidence from East Cornwall and elsewhere suggests that the exempt were likely to have accounted for around one-third of all households. This means that the number of families living in West Penwith when Charles II was king probably ranged between 1,050 and 1,150. We should add therefore about 350 households to those listed in 1664 for the missing exempt, all of whom we can assume had only one hearth each.

Three in four of all dwellings in West Penwith had only one hearth or fireplace, one in six had two hearths and one in ten between three and nine. None had ten hearths or more. A closer examination indicates two significant differences between the small town of Penzance and the surrounding countryside. Fewer than two-thirds of the households in Penzance had just one hearth, while one in five (or twice as many as in the rural area) had between three and nine.

The following extracts from the beginning and end of Gulval's assessment give a much clearer idea of what the hearth tax tells us:

GULVALL PARISHE 3,1

Christopher Harris Gen	xii	new built his house & hath but 9
John Hinson vic	iiii	Ex:
David Grosse gen	vi	Ex: now Mr Nich: Tresilian
George Veale Gent	vi	Ex:
William Donithorne	iiii	two fallen downe
John Friggens sen	ii	Ex:
Marten Martens	iii	now Rich: Harford hath one & ret one too many by mistake
Henry Fosse sen	ii	Ex:
Henry Fosse Jun	ii	Ex: now Eliz: Foll
Edward Downinge	ii	Ex:
Eliz: Newman wid:	i	Ex:
Richard Eva	i	Ex:

William Veale	i	Ex:
Richard Traveilor	i	Noe such person to be found
Marten Donn	ii	Ex: Avis Dunn

Justinian James	i	Ex: but very poore not rated etc by reson of poverty
Peter John	i	Ex:
Richard Veale	iiii	Ex:
William Visicke	iiii	one fallen downe
Pungo tenement	iiii	Ex:
Nicholas Fox	i	Ex: Hearthes not mencioned in the former returne
Richard Wallis	ii	
Richard Bennett	ii	
Henry Bone	i	
Anthony Quick	i	

The heading for the column of figures is 'Number of hearthes ret att Michaelmas 1662'. 'Ex:' is short for Examinatur, which means 'examined and found correct'. This confirmed that two years later the number of hearths was still the same so that where there was no 'Ex' they had changed. The comments refer to these or other changes that happened between 1662 and 1664. Thus Mr Harris reduced his house from 12 to 9 hearths by rebuilding it and two hearths or chimneys belonging to William Donithorne and one to William Visicke had fallen down. Somewhat suspiciously, six households in Gulval were recorded like these with fewer hearths and none had more; but in Madron eight were discovered to have returned one rather than two hearths and none claimed to have fewer.

David Grosse's, Henry Fosse junior's and Marten Donn's houses in Gulval had new occupants two years later. The parish register explains two of these changes and why Richard Traveilor cannot be found. In 1663 Henricus Fosse jun. was buried in June, Martinus Don in September and Richard Trevailer in February. Perhaps the Trevailer house was occupied by either Henry Bone or Anthony Quick nearly two years later. The entry for Marten Martens poses greater problems. Martinus Martin was buried on 16th September 1662, thirteen days before he was due to pay three shillings for his hearths. This may explain the 's' at the end of his surname, which we should probably interpret as Marten Marten's house. But it is not entirely clear what had happened to it by 1664. The entry claims it had only two hearths and not three, that Richard Harford had one of them, but there was no mention of the other. Had Martin Martin's house been split into two and was one half now empty or occupied by another Martin? The information provided here is insufficient to solve this problem.

Justinian James was one of the 23 householders who paid the tax in 1662, but was registered as exempt in 1664. The law concerning exemption was not straightforward; those whose rent was 20 shillings a year or less or whose house did not pay rates to the church and poor were covered by it so that James claimed exemption on the latter ground.

There are very few descriptions of the houses in which people lived. The only one that has survived for Gulval is the vicarage where John Hinson lived until his death in 1677. The **Glebe Terrier** of 1679 describes his four-hearth house as stone-walled and thatched (see chapter on Parsonages).

Parish registers have survived for all but two parishes (Sennen and St Levan) at West Penwith from the time of Charles II. Many are clearly not complete records of all the baptisms, marriages and burials, but nonetheless they provide much personal information about many families at this time.

While Schellinks was visiting Cornwall we know that William Hutchins, with a single hearth in St Buryan, was mourning his son Ralph who was buried on 10th August. In St Just, James and Katherine Warren (one hearth) had buried a still-born child on 25th July, while Richard Warren's four-hearth household still had fresh and painful memories of his son John, buried on 9th July.

On the other hand, the houses of Richard Eva and Richard Bennett in Gulval must have echoed to the cries of infant daughters baptised on 20th and 27th July. In Penzance Richard Saundry (1 hearth) also had a young daughter baptised at Madron on 20th July and Martin Gwennap's heavily pregnant wife gave birth about three weeks later in their three-hearth house to a son, who was baptised Martin on 14th August. Another Richard Bennett's family, with a one-hearth house in St Just, welcomed a baby who was christened Melchisadek on 21st September, but sadly young Melchisadek died before Christmas, less than three months old.

Wills and probate inventories
The wealthier usually drew up wills. Those that have survived often provide us with much information about the testators' family circumstances and their more treasured possessions just before they died. Historians in Cornwall are very fortunate because, unlike Devon, many wills are preserved in the County Record Office. In addition, most are accompanied by probate inventories which list the testators' belongings at the time of their deaths.

The Hearth Tax suggests that in the 1660s George Veale gentleman,[2] with six hearths, was one of Gulval's wealthiest inhabitants. This is confirmed by his will of August 1671 and his probate inventory, written two days after his burial in April 1672. George Veale's movable possessions, valued at £187, had the second highest total of the parish's 25 surviving inventories from the 1660s and 1670s. Although the £32 for his household goods accounted for only half of them, they were still Gulval's highest; presumably his wife or a son already owned the other half. His clothes were valued at £6. Farming provided the main source of George's personal wealth: his livestock totalled £115 (including 4 oxen, 6 steers, 10 kine and a bull for £47) and his crops £31, nearly twice as much as the next most valuable farm.

But his inventory provides only half the picture. George Veale's will reveals that he owned extensive property. He bequeathed to his wife and children at least thirteen houses with their related outbuildings and land etc in Penzance and Marazion and the parishes of Gulval, Madron, Ludgvan and Sithney. Because they were all let and his will mentioned the tenants' names, we know that one of these houses had six hearths, while four each had three, two and one hearths. In other words, most were quite substantial properties.

George Veale's will also reveals a lot about his immediate family just before he died. In 1671 his wife and three daughters were still living as well as seven sons, the youngest of whom was under 18 and the next youngest under 21. We know from the parish register that George and his wife had lost at least two children: a one year old son in 1658 and a 17 year old daughter in 1664. His eldest daughter and eldest son were both married; she had four children and he had only one, having lost two in 1666.

Because the eldest daughter was left only five shillings and the eldest son, William, just one, the same as each of George's servants, he may have provided for them both on their weddings, perhaps giving William the one-hearth house in which he lived. The only other child who did not receive any property was Tobyas, the third son, who got just ten pounds and may also have left home. There is no direct mention of the house where George Veale lived with his other children, but since he left the tenement of Rosemorran, which he leased, with all his estate therein to his second son, Richard, it could have been the family home.

George does not appear to have discriminated against his daughters or granddaughters, who received five shillings each just like his grandsons. His unmarried daughters were each left a property in Ludgvan and £30 or £10 on their wedding day, which for the younger one came a year after her father's death when she married a man from Marazion. The two youngest sons were to get a property in different parishes and £15 or £10 when they came of age. No other relative received a legacy, but his brother Richard of Gulval (with four hearths in 1664) was an overseer of his will. Perhaps he was also the father of the George Veale who accompanied William Schellinks around West Penwith in 1662, but unfortunately the parish register fails us at this stage because it only records two events for Richard's family: his marriage in 1637 and his wife's burial 32 years later.

References
1. Cornwall Hearth Tax 1664. PRO, E179/244/44
2. CRO V 196/1-2 George Veale
3. The Parish Registers of Gulval 1598-1812 ed. Millett and Bolitho, Penzance 1893

II SOME ONE HEARTH HOMES IN WEST PENWITH

IRIS M. GREEN

Records of a tax-raising measure of the government of Charles II, together with probate returns of some who lived in his reign (1660 - 1685) give an idea of homes of the time.

In the far western parishes of Sennen and St. Levan fifty-seven properties were examined but only forty-three were listed as liable for hearth tax in 1664. Apart from nine homes all were charged for one hearth, that is about eighty per cent. Pascho Tresillian of Raftra and John Bosustow of Higher Bosustow in St. Levan each had three hearths, though one in the latter property was 'stopt up'. In Sennen, Hugh Jones of Penrose Manor had four hearths and Pascho Ellis of Treveor had three. It would seem that by far the greater number of families lived in a one-hearth dwelling not regarded as taxable by reason of being valued at less than twenty shillings per year, or occupied by a person not liable for church or poor rates. These untaxed homes may have represented a further half or more of housing stock.

As illustrated in the bar-graph below the situation in the town of Penzance, ten miles away, was vastly different.

Moreover, far fewer than half the houses examined in Penzance were listed for tax. Of the one hundred and one appearing on the tax list, forty-one had one hearth. Other homes boasted from two to nine hearths, though it was probable that some of these were lived in by several families.

It might be imagined that the one-hearth home would be a standard one-storeyed thatched building consisting of a single room (of varying size) with a central fire and a hole above for the escape of smoke, or with a hearth and chimney on one lateral wall. One example is in Treen farmyard, St. Levan, where a building, now used for livestock, measuring about twenty-five by forty-five feet has a tiny hearth and bread oven at one end.

On the other hand, an inventory shows that the one-hearth house of yeoman James Cara, who died in 1667 and lived at the main Treen Farm, consisted of a hall for sleeping and living, a well-equipped kitchen for the time and a 'new house'. The new house seems to have been an additional room for storage or living in, or both. It may well have been a shippon or cow-house converted to domestic use when it became usual to winter animals out-of-doors in this mild area of the country. The dimensions and appearance of a present-day milking parlour at Ardensawah (St. Levan) suggest that it was once the three-roomed farmhouse here. It has the carved, coiled-stone-kneeler decoration at the roof-line found also in a grander building such as Pendeen Manor (Plate 4), or at Roskestal in St. Levan, where the 1677 farmhouse (remodelled in 1730) is at right angles to a much earlier simple house.

A CARVED KNEELER AT MORVAH

The Ardensawah farmhouse was lived in by a literate tenant farming family until at least 1763. Alexander Dennis, author of *Journal of a Tour (1810)* was born to this family in 1739 and continued at the farm until he was old enough to take his own tenancy in Trembath, near Newlyn.

The term 'new house' was used in two further St. Levan inventories at the end of the 17th. century, but it has not been found in Sennen records. In one of these St. Levan farmhouses at Trengothal, yeoman Francis Wallish, recorded as having one hearth in 1664, but not dying until 1697 had, in addition to hall, kitchen and new house, a dispense or buttery and a chamber with additional beds. It is possible that the buttery and upper room may have been built on between 1664 and 1697, but the form of the inventory, by its mention of 'new house', is some indication that he may well have been living in a pre-1664 farmhouse at his death.

One hearth cottage (in shell form)

In the parish of Sennen, three yeoman farmers and a husbandman, two of whom were very comfortably off, and the third not poor, died between 1661 and 1667. Two, and in the other case a successor, lived in one-hearth houses in 1664. The inventory of John Richards, whose tenement was at Treveor, mentions bed, cupboard, press and chest in the hall and all the equipment for food preparation and eating in the kitchen. The list of his household goods continues with two more beds, a spinning 'turne' (wheel), and barrels and tubs, so perhaps these were in a third room, either adjoining or above the kitchen.

Thomas Harvye lived in a one-hearth house at Mayon. He had grants of five estates of land, making him a wealthy man. His inventory gives the contents of his kitchen and suggests that the rest of his almost £30 worth of household goods were in one or two further rooms.

In 1688 the household goods of Matthew Williams were listed under hall, kitchen and chamber over kitchen, the latter containing a small bed and chest. The word 'chamber' implies an upper room. This may have been added after 1664, but there is no reason to think that another hearth was also added. An upper sleeping chamber would not require heating. The 1661 inventory of Edmond Nicholas of Trevillie mentions chamber and hall separately and a further room or rooms with more beds, table-board, andirons and spits in addition to weaving looms and other equipment in the shop. In his chamber, which was the main bedroom, there was a 'drilled chair'. This is not a standard term, but may have been a 'turned' chair in which holes were drilled in the seat to take the turned members of the back.[1] Edmond bequeathed this house to his son, William, who was named on the hearth tax-list with one hearth.

Yeoman farmers of Sennen seem to have been more prosperous than those of St. Levan. Inventories of four Sennen farmers mention 'wool in the house', John Richards had 'fleeces of wool' and Edmond Nicholas twenty pounds of wool and eighteen pounds of 'thrums', the fringe of threads at the edges of pieces of cloth. As well as being a farmer, he was a weaver with a pair of weaving looms in his shop. Both these men had a spinning 'turne'. The importance of sheep and associated industries is dealt with elsewhere in this book. Fishing may have supplemented the income of Martin Williams who had the hull of a boat and its implements, and of John Williams who had ropes, lines and fish-hooks. However, the high inventory totals of John Richards, Edmond Nicholas and Thomas Harvye are largely explained by the leases they held. On the other hand, the products of arable, and to a lesser extent dairy and beef farming, seem to have been the only other assets of St. Levan yeoman.

Thus, from the evidence available, it would seem that the seventeenth century one-hearth house in St. Levan and Sennen, home to husbandmen and yeoman farmers with a 99-year lease, generally consisted of one or two rooms with an adjoining store and/or living space. Three examples show the creation of one, almost certainly unheated, upper room.

A similar study of probate records for Penzance has been more limited. Probate returns for half the occupants of one-hearth houses are available for St. Levan and Sennen, but in Penzance only three out of forty remain for the years 1674 to 1681.

The inventory of Thomas Fynny, a tanner, is not arranged by rooms but the simple possessions of the widower suggest a one or two-roomed building with a working store area housing leather, hides, horse and calves' skins which formed the bulk of his wealth.

Widow Blanch George lived in a house with a hall, buttery, a chamber in which she slept and a kitchen. The hall contained a chair, dishes, flagons and candlesticks. No doubt, the hearth was here. A pan, crock, old kieves and tubs were in the kitchen.

The inventory of William Som(m)ers, gentleman, detailing his ten-roomed house and cellar suggests he is not the man listed on the tax list with one hearth, but the son of a father of the same name. A study of parish records, however, does not reveal another person.

He was a candle-maker with candles and scales in his shop and tallow, wool yarn and 'other materials belonging hereunto' in his workhouse. The equipment for making barrels and salting fish was in his cellar and he had a boat and nets. He had two chattel estates, one in Tredavoe near Newlyn. The other lease was for his house, garden and cellar in Penzance in which he lived, together with another small house and one meadow. He was not a land-<u>owner.</u> The title of 'gentleman' has been found elsewhere, given to a man in old age able to live on his past earnings.

A HEARTH - WELL FURNISHED.

The ground floor of William Somer's house consisted of hall, shop, buttery (a store room for liquor and food), kitchen and workhouse. Above each of these was another room. Only in the kitchen were the objects associated with a wall hearth - a pair of andirons which were horizontal bars supported on three short feet, placed on each side of the hearth to support burning wood; a spit which was thrust through meat for roasting before a fire, with a dripping pan below; a gridiron, which was a platform consisting of iron bars with short feet and a long handle, for cooking meat over a fire, and an iron tripod on which to hang cooking vessels over the fire, known as a brandish.

The hall contained table, stools, chairs and cupboards only, but in the five upper rooms were eight beds. Did he also provide accommodation for visiting seafarers or travellers? His house may well have been in that part of Penzance near the shore called The Greens and now known as Battery Rocks where much property has been cleared. Despite his many rooms, the value of his household goods was little more than half that of Thomas Harvye of Sennen.

These examples of homes with one room or ten, one storey or two between a thatched roof and earthen or flag-stone floor, could each exist with one open fire - a one-hearth house. Although methods and appliances have changed, it has taken until the mid-twentieth century to develop the concept of total house heating.

Valuations of household goods in one-hearth houses

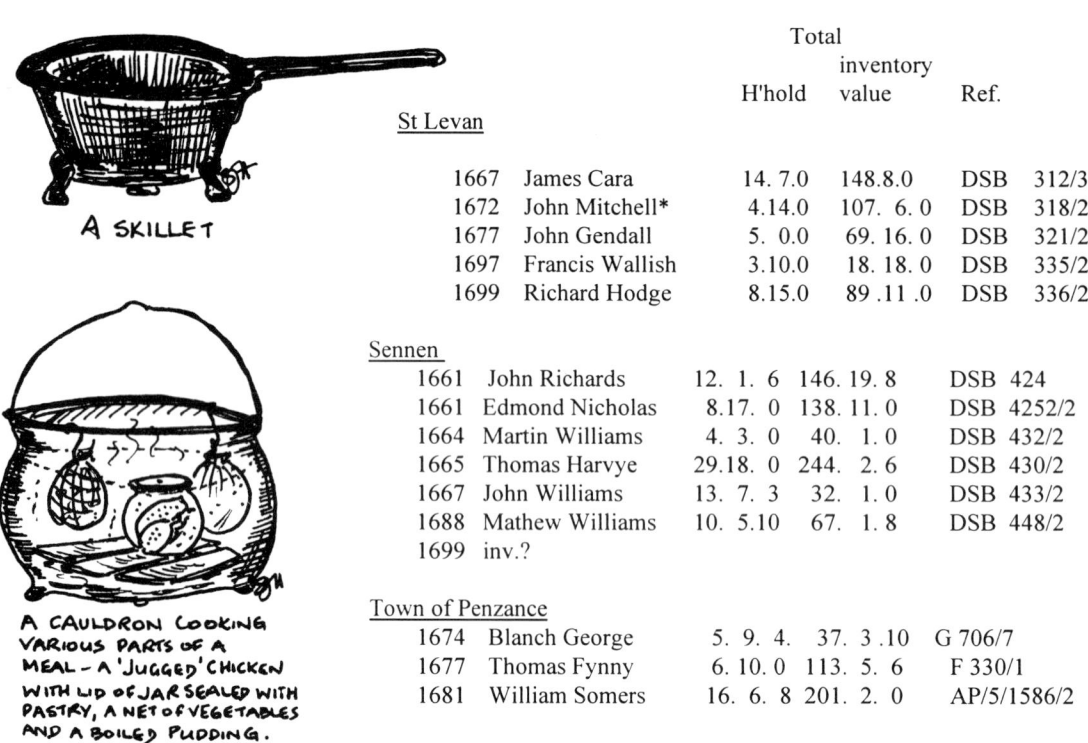

A SKILLET

A CAULDRON COOKING VARIOUS PARTS OF A MEAL - A 'JUGGED' CHICKEN WITH LID OF JAR SEALED WITH PASTRY, A NET OF VEGETABLES AND A BOILED PUDDING.

			H'hold	Total inventory value	Ref.	
St Levan						
	1667	James Cara	14. 7.0	148.8.0	DSB	312/3
	1672	John Mitchell*	4.14.0	107. 6. 0	DSB	318/2
	1677	John Gendall	5. 0.0	69. 16. 0	DSB	321/2
	1697	Francis Wallish	3.10.0	18. 18. 0	DSB	335/2
	1699	Richard Hodge	8.15.0	89 .11 .0	DSB	336/2
Sennen						
	1661	John Richards	12. 1. 6	146. 19. 8	DSB	424
	1661	Edmond Nicholas	8.17. 0	138. 11. 0	DSB	4252/2
	1664	Martin Williams	4. 3. 0	40. 1. 0	DSB	432/2
	1665	Thomas Harvye	29.18. 0	244. 2. 6	DSB	430/2
	1667	John Williams	13. 7. 3	32. 1. 0	DSB	433/2
	1688	Mathew Williams	10. 5.10	67. 1. 8	DSB	448/2
	1699	inv.?				
Town of Penzance						
	1674	Blanch George	5. 9. 4.	37. 3 .10	G 706/7	
	1677	Thomas Fynny	6. 10. 0	113. 5. 6	F 330/1	
	1681	William Somers	16. 6. 8	201. 2. 0	AP/5/1586/2	

Probate returns - C.R.O. Truro   * Some family documents use the spelling Michell

As can be seen, there was considerable variation in the value of household goods within these homes. Relative wealth alone does not explain this. Family size and age had an effect. John Mitchell, a childless widower of Cheurgwin (Chegwidden), St. Levan, with the second highest inventory valuation, had reduced his possessions to one each of bed, pan, cauldron, brass crock, iron crock, table-board, charra (chair), form, coffer and chest. He was the only one with a cauldron. This was a large cooking pot with a lid and handle which could be suspended over a fire. Meat in a small crock, vegetables in a net and

14

perhaps a pudding in a pudding-cloth, could be simmered in one operation. This would be economical and convenient for a busy tenant farmer without a wife. James Cara, on the other hand was a yeoman of similar status, with a wife and two daughters. He had beds, bedstead, bedclothes, crocks, pans and chairs in the plural as well as candlesticks, dishes, trenchers, spits, andirons and pewter.

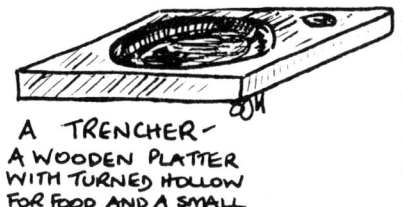

A TRENCHER - A WOODEN PLATTER WITH TURNED HOLLOW FOR FOOD AND A SMALL SIDE HOLE FOR SALT.

The womenfolk looked after the turning and basting of the fish, poultry or meat on the spit. Early trenchers were of square-cut wholemeal bread but these were now replaced by wooden, or occasionally pewter, trenchers. The wooden square board would have a central hollow for meat and gravy, while a smaller hollow in one corner was for salt. Mention of a salt or salt-cellar is made only in the inventories of John Richards of Sennen and Thomas Fynny of Penzance.

Francis Wallish, an old man previously mentioned, had made over the lands he owned to his daughter before his death. Freehold land was not recorded in inventories. The household goods in his five-roomed house were of low value, though he could not be regarded as poor. Thomas Harvye of Sennen had similar possessions, but more of them and of superior quality. His four bedsteads, feather beds, bedclothes and bedsheets were valued at £12, twice that of gentleman Richard Bosustow in 1707. John Mitchell's bed was valued at £1.

Most inventories list cooking vessels and containers but brandish, spit and andirons are mentioned in one house in St. Levan, four in Sennen and two in the one-hearth inventories from Penzance. Perhaps these homes as well as that of John Mitchell, had their hearth on a lateral wall, rather than the centre of the hall.

No 'luxury' items were noted in St. Levan inventories but in Sennen five yeoman farmers owned between them thirty-one silver spoons. Mention is also made of linen, table-cloths and napkins, clomen (earthenware) jugs and carpets which were covers for the table. The lanthorne was a portable light with metal walls and panels of horn enclosing a candle.

Widow Blanch George had canvas (coarse linen or hemp) sheets and napkins, a board cloth and four towels. Dishes, plates, porringers (bowls for soup or porridge), flagons, kieves, tubs and pinters feature conspicuously in her inventory. Did she keep an ale-house? The luxury in William Somers' house was curtains and vallances around two of his beds, giving some protection in unheated rooms.

STEADBED WITH CURTAINS AND VALLANCE

Beds were important. The simplest found in these inventories was the flock bed (stuffed with lumpy ends of unspun wool) and feather bed, both of which would lie on the floor unless it was stated that they were on a stead bed (bedstead). The trundle or truckle bed was on wheels. It could be pushed under a high or standing bed when not in use. A half bed is also mentioned. John Richards and Blanch George both had field beds which were camp or trestle bedsteads used in the open air as well as in the house. In John Richards' case this indicated his need to sleep out when moving livestock, particularly sheep, to summer pastures and the scattered nature of his land holdings.

Finally, in all the parishes west of Penzance, between sixty and sixty-five per cent of those taxed in 1664 were assessed on one hearth, but this did not necessarily reflect poverty of these occupants. The average inventory valuation of St. Levan men was £86; those in Sennen £111. Even if their chattel leases are not included, these figures become £43 and £59 respectively. A survey of 150 probate records in

Cambridgeshire of the 16th and 17th centuries gives the average wealth of those living in a one-hearth house as £25.[2] It is unfortunate that more probate returns for occupiers in one-hearth homes in Penzance are not available in order to see whether these match findings for the city of York in the 17th century where 'the number of hearths was a reasonably accurate indicator of the number of rooms in a dwelling which could in turn be interpreted as an expression of the wealth or prosperity of the occupier'.[3] This certainly does not apply in the West Penwith examples studied here. In the last half of the seventeenth century, 'the great majority of people lived in houses with only one fireplace, but they must not be dismissed simply as the rural proletariat'.[4]

References
1. Furniture History Society
2. English Local History. Kate Tiller. 1992 (Statistics from Contrasting Communities- English Villagers in the 16th and 17th Centuries) Margaret Spufford. 1974. Alan Sutton
3. Data-linkage and the Hearth Tax : the case of 17th century York. Deborah Hibberd. 1983
4. Local History in England. W.G. Hoskins. 1959. Longman
   English Historical Documents Vol. VIII. ed. A. Browning. 1966. Eyre and Spottiswoode
   A Glossary of Household, Farming and Trade Terms from Probate Inventories. Rosemary Milward 1986. Derbyshire Record Society
   Food and Cooking in 16th and 17th Century Britain. Peter Brears. 1985. English Heritage

HEARTH AND SPIT WITH DRIPPING PANS BELOW

III THE PARSON'S EVIDENCE

VERONICA CHESHER

Introduction.

One of the most important and tantalising questions raised by the Hearth Tax returns is what do the number of hearths tell us about the houses and the rooms they had. What were the overall standards and housing stock in West Penwith in the second half of the 17th century?

Answers can be pursued in a wide range of evidence which at some date needs to include a detailed survey of surviving buildings. Probate inventories are a rich source of information, even allowing for the pitfalls of interpretation. Less well known are glebe terriers, or descriptions of church property by the parish priests * (also illustration page 77).

In these returns we hear the voice of parsons describing their houses. We learn of building materials, the number and type of rooms, often their actual layout. We glimpse details such as plastered or lime-washed walls, planched ceilings, floors of beaten earth, limeash or, less often, boards. The scene outside is set with vegetable, flower and herb gardens, barns, stables and outbuildings in the townplace (farmyard). Beyond them are orchards, meadows, the pasture and arable of the glebe land. The breadth of information and detail, together with the idiosyncrasies of the incumbents make glebe terriers a particularly lively and rounded source for study of this category of 17th - 18th century houses.

The terriers most relevant to the Hearth Tax returns are those of 1679/80 and survive for six parishes in West Penwith. The terriers of 1727/8 amend and enlarge the picture.

The Glebe Terriers

<u>Gulval.</u> *Hall floored, stone walled, thatched. Kitchen likewise. Buttery floored, stone walled with chamber over, white limed. Entry with little chamber over, white limed, walls of both stone. Outer dairy floored, stone walled, thatched....*

Gulval parish lies to the immediate east of Penzance and its churchtown has sweeping views across Mount's Bay. Mr. Phillip Hicks' vicarage was a modest one and old fashioned with no mention of a chamber over the hall indicating a medieval type hall which was open to the roof timbers and used as a living-room. He had no parlour or more private living quarters. A buttery supplemented the kitchen and the outer dairy may have been a later addition, as it was in many 17th century west country farmhouses. Upstairs the bedroom accommodation was noticeably meagre. The little chamber over the entry (which was the passage through the house) was a favourite location for the parson's study. The dairy excepted, no outbuildings were mentioned but a stable appeared in the 1727 terrier. Around the

SPARR THATCH - THATCH 'PINNED' IN PLACE

house were two gardens and a mowhay, or rick yard. Beyond were sixteen or so acres of glebe which included four arable fields and two meadows. No orchard was mentioned in 1679 but by 1727 there was one with 50 trees. By then a neighbour had encroached upon the glebe and planted 100 cherry trees for which he paid in fruit. The terrier of 1727 states that the parsonage was lately 'mostly' built by the incumbent. It had two principal ground floor rooms, uses unspecified. Two little rooms were secondary service rooms in a lean-to on the side, or more probably at the rear of the house. It seems there was a complete upper floor of three bedchambers, a study, probably over the entry, and two little linney rooms.

Ludgvan. *Hall, floored, stone walled, roofed with heling stone (slate). Parlour, planched, stone walled; chamber above roofed with heling stone. Kitchen, floored; chamber above, stone walled, thatched. Little parlour, floored, buttery within it, chamber above, stone walled, thatched. Porch with little chamber over, walls plastered, roofed with heling stone. Entry with study and closet over, stone walled, roofed with heling stone....*

At Ludgvan, a few miles east of Gulval, Mr. Samuel Davyes lived in a considerably better residence as befitted his status as rector. He had extensive accommodation with two parlours in addition to the hall, and five chambers upstairs with a study. One of the chambers was over what must have been a storeyed porch. The kitchen quarters were supplemented not only by a buttery and cellar in the house with a brewhouse, bakehouse and washhouse, probably outside in a kitchen court. The interior detail of the house was also superior to that at Gulval, with planked floors (planched) in the parlours and plaster walls in the porch chamber. There is no mention of a room above the hall. Do we assume that the Ludgvan parson's house, like Gulval's, retained its open medieval hall? It seems to have been in an older block, distinct from that containing the little parlour, buttery and kitchen quarters. The gardens around the house were two small 'apple gardens' with about 50 trees, and a kitchen garden. The 25 acres of glebe were served by a stable, barn and poultry and pig houses. The terrier of 1727 mentions 'homestead' (farmyard), mowhay and dung court and also a court before the house, and describes the glebe land as being five arable fields and three furze crofts 'called the Sentrys' (from the word sanctuary, signifying church land).

By 1727 the house was modernised, at least as far as the names and uses of rooms were concerned. There was a 'little hall' possibly an entrance lobby and 'a large hall or kitchen', a parlour, and a Higher Parlour within the hall, 'now a lodging room', that is for sleeping. There were also five bedchambers above. Outside were an outer kitchen with chamber above and a dairy; these seem to have replaced the brewhouse, bakehouse and washhouse of 1680. The fact that the Reverend William Borlase was rector by then might explain the improvements, given the social status and wealth of the Borlase family and the wide interests of that eminent scholar.

Paul. *'The Antient house belonging to the sayd vicaridge consistinge of many Rooms was wholely burnt and demolished by Certaine Spanish Invaders aboute the yeare 1595, of which sayd house some parte was Reedifyed and some parte left ever since in the Ruines. Which sayd house soe reedifyed Consistinge of Convenient Roomes for A Vicar's habitation before the late troubles by the civill wars grew into Some decay. And, in the sayd troubles the then vicar being sequesterd and Removed it became wholely Ruinous and dilapidated and so Remained to the present Incumbents Induction into the sd Vicaridge.'*

Mr. John Smith, the incumbent making this doleful statement, went on to report that he had at his own expense repaired two rooms on the ground floor - the kitchen and a room adjoining at the west end, both thatched. Outside were three gardens and a little court with 'waste places to make fuel on'. These, with the old walls and ruins only amounted to half an acre contained in a triangular plot narrowing towards the east.

By 1727 the Vicar, Henry Pendarves, reported that the house was recently rebuilt. At last the vicarage provided a comfortable home with five ground rooms, each about 14 feet square and six chambers and a study - ample accommodation by the standards of Penwith parsonages of the time. One room had a deal floor and the remainder were floored with beaten earth. By then the whole house was roofed with slate although a stable outside was thatched. One of the gardens had become a small orchard but the whole glebe still only amounted to half an acre and 'without commons'.

Sancreed. *Entry. Hall with chamber over. Parlour with chamber over. Buttery and Dairy with chamber above. Kitchen....*

Sancreed parish and its churchtown lie some miles northwest of Paul in the central uplands of West Penwith. Here John Smyth, vicar, compiled a terrier in 1672/3, seven years earlier than the principal collection of 1680. The house he described was typical of the medium-sized Cornish house of the mid to later 17th century, with through-passage, hall used as a living-room, second living-room (parlour) and kitchen and ancillary domestic rooms. All had chambers above except the kitchen, which was possibly in a rear lean-to. There was a court in front of the house and another behind; also a townplace (farmyard), a mowhay, a yard for fuel and a sheepfold. There were two gardens and an orchard. Farm buildings consisted of a barn, stable, and two other outbuildings (one was described as a poultry house in 1727). The land comprised about twenty nine acres of meadow, arable and pasture with additional rough pasture unenclosed in 'a great down about forty acres'.

Fifty years later there was an 'improving' parson at Sancreed. He rebuilt the house, giving it four ground floor rooms (two of which had deal floors) and five chambers above. He also planted about sixty apple trees in the orchard and a dozen or so ash trees in the churchyard. Although he was vicar, not rector, he noted that the vicarage was endowed with the great tithes of the Manor of Gwiddn, Trerice and Nuham in Sancreed. Perhaps these extra resources helped to pay for his new house.

<u>Zennor.</u> *(Undated but apparently 1680) Hall, Milkhouse, both earth floored. Kitchen, earth floored. Two chambers over the hall....*
Anthony Rondell, the vicar, described the whole house as stone walled and sparr thatched. There was an outhouse, 're-edified by one Madderne, deceased.' All the accommodation downstairs had earth floors. The parsonage stood close to the church on the plateau above the storm-swept northwest coastline of West Penwith with the parish land running up to the downs on the south.

The glebe included a garden in the praze or meadow leading to the sea and a mowhay. The modest size of the parsonage, compared with Sancreed's, was reflected in the equally modest glebeland estimated in 1727 as about ten acres. The house described by John Oliver in 1727, seems to have shrunk as it contained only two ground floor rooms and two chambers, but the roof was `sparr thatched'. However, a stable and barn outside, which like the house contained three bays of building, included a large chimney and oven which presumably served as an outside kitchen or bakehouse.

<u>St. Just.</u> *Hall, Kitchen, Buttery or Cellar, Milkhouse or Dairy; Three Chambers....*
St. Just is the penultimate parish before Land's End, on the north west coast of West Penwith. It has a long connection with the tin industry. However the terriers suggest only limited resources as far as parsonage and glebe were concerned. In 1679 Mr. James Millett complained that his house was 'very ruinous, covered with healing, the walls of stone, but both Roof and Walls much impaired by reason of the long growth of Ivy thereon, through the carelessness and neglect of my predecessor, who held it nigh fourty years and not yet rectified by the present incumbent, the profits of his Vicarridge being small, and hee under first fruits but intended with all speed possible as soon as God shall enable him'.

Outside, probably at the rear of the house, was a second kitchen, a stable and barn, all stone walled. Mr. Millett noted that their roofs were of 'roapstraw thatch'. There was a kitchen garden of twenty laces (landyards) and a flower garden of ten laces. The glebe was small; eight acres in four small enclosures with a townplace. In 1728 James Millett, still in occupation, commented in his terrier that these glebelands were sufficient for four cows, a horse and tillage of two and a half acres. By then he had repaired (or rebuilt) the

SMALL ROPED-THATCH COTTAGE
-THATCH HELD BY ROPE 'NET'
WEIGHTED BY ROCKS.

house, which he described as being of solid stone with a slate roof, measuring about 40 feet by 20 feet. It had five ground floor rooms, an entry passage and a staircase leading to five chambers and a closet. His flower and kitchen gardens were still there and he had enclosed three small plots for tilling roots, presumably squeezed out of his meagre glebeland. His barn included a malthouse. After signing his name in 1728 Mr. Millett added "aetatis sua 80". One of the churchwardens who signed was a James Millett and among parishioners signing was a Martin Millett. By that time, the Milletts were obviously a well-established St. Just family and parson Millett quite an institution in the parish.

Summary and Discussion

These descriptions of West Penwith parsons' homes contain a mass of evidence about the houses as well as their surrounding outbuilding and land. What overall picture emerges of the parsonages and of house types across the peninsula?

The first noticeable fact about the parsonages was their variety. By 1727 Zennor and Gulval were the smallest, each with two rooms to a floor. What significance is there that both seem to have shrunk since 1680? Ludgvan in 1680 had the amplest accommodation with its three living rooms and four domestic rooms on the ground floor and five chambers and a study above; supplementing this was the brewhouse, bakehouse and washhouse. Its porch with a room above gave it something approaching gentry status. The parson at Sancreed was reasonably well provided for, with two living rooms and three domestic rooms. At St. Just the vicar had to be content with a hall used as a living room, a kitchen and two other service rooms with a second kitchen outside. By 1727 James Millett at St. Just had enlarged his house upstairs and down. The new built parsonage at Sancreed had one less room on the ground floor, unless the 'buttery and dairy' in 1680 was one room.

Overall there are signs of improvement by the early 18th century in West Penwith. Ludgvan was the most interesting example with a new style hall-entrance lobby by 1727 and the old hall becoming a kitchen. This relegation of the medieval hall in name and function is a trend which occurred widely in Cornish terriers of the time and is accompanied by a good deal of confusion in nomenclature. The medieval style hall, unceiled and with no room above, was on its way out: this occurred at Ludgvan and in the more modest house at Gulval (and probably St. Just). The new built house at Paul also had a full upper floor. Sancreed and Zennor already had chambers over their halls by 1680.

As far as interior finish was concerned, there are a few signs of improving parsons at work on their houses. Most of the parsonages in 1680 had little in the way of interior decor and finish if the negative evidence in the terriers is to be accepted. Ludgvan had the luxury of a board floor parlour in 1680; by 1727 its two parlours were planched while the hall and kitchen had limeash floors. The new house at Gulval in 1727 had one room planched and the lately built parsonage at Paul had a room with a floor specifically designated as 'deal'. Two out of four of Sancreed's ground floor rooms had deal floors. Such floors were definitely considered improvements with status. Many Cornish parsons were installing them although some were laid direct on to the 'country' bringing disastrous rotting later.

There is little detail on interior wall treatment although Gulval had two chambers white limed in 1680. At Paul there is the negative information in 1727 that no rooms are wainscotted (panelled) or ceiled. Ludgvan again led the way with the porch chamber plastered in 1680 and both parlours given plastered walls by 1727.

As far as structural building materials are concerned, there is much more information. The overall picture is the preponderance of stone for walling, no doubt from the granite uplands. St. Just had 'solid stone walls'. The only mention of cob was in outbuildings at Ludgvan in 1680. This suggests that cob was mainly found in inferior or older buildings. The same might be asserted as far as thatch was concerned. Slate roofs tended to predominate, particularly on newer buildings. In 1680, the old house at Paul was thatched but the replacement described in 1727 was slated as was the new house at Sancreed. In both cases outbuildings were thatched. The same occurred at St. Just and Ludgvan where in 1680 the main part of the house was slated and what could have been an older part was thatched. This combination of materials was also reported in 1727, the terriers suggesting variations in thatching materials. At Paul the parson describes his stable roof as reed thatched; the parsonage house at Zennor was 'spar thatched' while the vicar of St. Just, in both the 1680 and 1727 terriers, spoke of straw rope thatch on his outbuildings.

Does all this information throw light on houses generally across the peninsula in the period? It does for a number of reasons and one is the variety of houses in the terriers. It is a variety which is found right across the spectrum of parsonages in Cornwall and must reflect the more general picture of contemporary Cornish rural house types. This is supported by surviving examples of the period. The two or three room plan in a rectangular building with cross passage entry giving access at front and rear, with extra domestic accommodation in a rear court or in a lean-to along the back of the house, is recognisable in many terriers.

Another strong reason for seeing the Penwith parsonages as types of local houses generally is that in rural Cornwall the parson's lifestyle had much in common with his parishioners. Like many of them, he held land and farmed it. In the terriers he had barns, shippons, pig and poultry houses as well as a stable for his nag. He also had a farmyard, mowhay and 'a place to make fuel in'.

If the parsons' houses reflect local house types, were the tentative improvements they were making part of a general phase of upgrading domestic accommodation? The descriptions of listed buildings in West Penwith show innumerable houses which were added to or improved internally in the eighteenth century. In many cases this was happening rather later than the period of the terriers. Perhaps the movement gained momentum as the development of the tin industry in the area also gained momentum and brought new wealth. There is also architectural evidence of house improvement earlier in Penwith. At Pendeen (Plate 4), the ancestral home of the Borlase family appears to have been enlarged and improved during the seventeenth century. An example in a more modest house is Rissick in St. Buryan where there were two building periods in the seventeenth century. Does this indicate a high proportion of small and simple houses, as suggested by the Hearth Tax returns, resulting in a first phase of improvements?

This brings us back to the tantalising problem of relating Hearth Tax returns to house types. As far as the parsonages in the terriers are concerned, four can definitely be linked to a return. The parson at Gulval returned four hearths, which could be ones in hall, kitchen and two chambers. Sancreed also returned four - in hall, parlour, kitchen and perhaps one of the two chambers above. Zennor only returned two, presumably in hall and kitchen. Ludgvan, much grander in all respects, returned ten hearths, which is difficult to equate with hall, two parlours, kitchen and four principle chambers, unless the cellar and the little room over the porch were included. All this indicates the caution needed in relating hearth numbers to house types, particularly in this case where there is a lapse of twenty years between the tax returns and the terriers. One interesting point is that it was not unusual to have fireplaces in parsonage bedchambers by then. In Cornwall this seems most common in gentry houses of the time. Were Cornish parsons emerging from their rather indeterminate social position progressing towards the more established status of a century or so later? Be that as it may, the types and sizes of houses in these late seventeenth and early eighteenth century terriers, taken in context, suggest a wide social spectrum in a study of local domestic architecture. These were the kind of houses lived in by parishioners as well as parsons in contemporary West Penwith.

* For a full discussion of Glebe Terriers and their origins see the introduction to A Calendar of Cornish Glebe Terriers 1673-1735 (edited by Richard Potts, Devon and Cornwall Record Society 1974). The Calendar is an essential aid to the study of Cornish parsonages and Cornish domestic architecture of the period.

CRO ARD/TER/501 Gulval 1679
CRO ARD/TER/655 Ludgvan 1727
CRO ARD/TER387 Sancreed 1680
ARD/TER/704 Zennor 1727
CRO ARD/TER/502 Gulval 1727
CRO ARD/TER350 Paul 1680
CRO ARD/TER/571 Sancreed 1727
CRO ARD/TER/245 St. Just 1679
CRO ARD/TER/299 Ludgvan 1680
CRO ARD/TER/558 Paul 1727
CRO ARD/TER/445 Zennor (undated) CRO
CRO ARD/TER/245 St. Just 1728

IV HOUSEHOLD GOODS FROM PROBATE INVENTORIES

TOM ARKELL

Their total value

The number of hearths listed for taxation purposes gives only a broad indication of each household's economic standing. Three in four families living in West Penwith had only one hearth, but some of these lived much more comfortably than others. The total value of each probate inventory was not always a reliable indicator of the deceased's wealth for several reasons. Some inventories were drawn up more carefully than others and some omitted any possessions that had been bequeathed. As we have seen with George Veale (chapter I) they covered only movable goods and not real estate. For such reasons, the total value of the household goods often gives a better indicator of a family's standard of living. Also, when an inventory lists the deceased's furniture and household equipment in considerable detail, it provides an even clearer insight into differing lifestyles.

Most of the more detailed inventories that have survived for Penzance and the eleven parishes of West Penwith from the 1660s and 1670s have been studied. They are virtually confined to the middle ranks of society and the better off. Inventories were rarely made for those with possessions worth less than five pounds and so even more of the poorer households were omitted than from the Hearth Tax. Because those with household goods worth less than two pounds very rarely occupied whole houses, they have not been included in the following analysis. It seems most belonged to widowed or single people who occupied a room or two within a larger dwelling or just had a few prized possessions.

The accompanying table shows that five in six of the 153 deceased in West Penwith had household goods valued between two and twenty pounds and a mere one in six had twenty pounds worth or more. This higher category contained just one in sixteen of the female heads of households, virtually all of whom were widows.

Value of household goods

Parish	Total h'holds	£2-5	£6-10	£11-19	£20-29	£30-49	£50-99	£100+
Men								
Gulval	16	6	5	3	1	1	-	-
Madron	18	6	8	3	1	-	-	-
Penzance	20	1	9	5	2	1	2	-
Morvah, Zennor & Towednack	14	8	3	3	-	-	-	-
Paul & Sancreed	17	7	7	2	1	-	-	-
Sennen & St Levan	14	6	-	5	2	1	-	-
St Buryan	17	6	5	2	-	1	2	1
St Just	21	5	6	3	3	1	1	2
All men	137	45	43	26	10	5	5	3
All women	16	7	4	4	1	-	-	-
Total	153	52	47	30	11	5	5	3

COOPERAGE - WOODEN TUBS AND HOOPED VESSELS

The occupation or status of the deceased men is recorded in three-fifths of these inventories. In Penzance the two wealthiest were merchants, while those with household goods between five and ten pounds were craftsmen, such as tanners, carpenters and a potter. In the countryside those with over £30 who were given a status or occupation were all gentlemen, but a single gentleman was also found in each of the lower sub-categories in our table. There the recorded husbandmen had between three and six pounds, tinners between two and seven pounds, a mason, labourer and fuller between three and five pounds and a butcher, tailor and blacksmith between eight and eleven pounds of household goods. The distribution of the yeomen's possessions was quite different. Yeomen are often assumed to have been the wealthiest farmers, but in fact the name was in part a status title for those below the gentry. This explains why two-thirds of those with between five and thirty pounds of household goods were yeomen as well as half of those with between two and five pounds.

Writing a probate inventory

The best probate inventories were written with great care a few days after the deceased's death, normally by two or three neighbours who acted as appraisers. Often they listed and valued in great detail the furniture and equipment in the dwelling and, where appropriate, the deceased's crops, livestock and trade goods. When studied together, the best inventories reveal much about the household possessions and living standards of the gentry and middle orders. In the larger houses the appraisers normally noted each room with the goods in them, but in West Penwith most houses had so few rooms that they rarely needed to name each one to ensure they had covered the whole house.

When the rooms are listed, we can easily imagine ourselves following the appraisers around the house as they carried out their task. Two months after Charles II was restored to the throne, Charles Ellis died in July 1660 at Brea farmhouse,[1] which still stands on the Sennen side of Land's End airport. His son John, one of the earliest Quakers, inherited this property. Charles Ellis was clearly a wealthy man because his probate inventory totalled £350[1]. His wearing apparel was valued at £6, his plate at £12 and his household linen at £6. In the house items were listed according to the rooms where they were found. The unusual ones are explained in the glossary at the end of the book.

'*In the Chamber over the Parlour:* One great bedsteede, one Trundle bed, both Furnished, One table Board & Carpett & Cushiones with other nessesaryes to the sayd Chamber belongeinge £11

In the Chamber over the Hall: One Bedsteed Furnished, one table board & Carpett & all other necessaryes to the sayd Chamber belongeinge £4

In the Littel Chamber: One Bead & Bedsteed Furnished £2 10s

In the Chamber over the kitchin: Two Beds & Beadsteedes Furnished with Deale boardes & all other Boardes in the sayd Chamber & *the loft over* and lether with other implements £9

In two little Roomes over the Kittchen £1 10s

In the Chamber over the stayres: Two Dosen & tenn Pewter Platters, one Ewer, three Pewter Chamber Pots, two brasse Candelstickes, Fower Dosen of trenchares & other necessaryes in the sayd Chamber £3

In the Parlour: One bed & Bedsteed Furnished, One table board and Carpet & Cushiones, one Chest, three Chaires, one forme, one Joynt stoole, one Cradle £4

In the Hall: One table board & carpett, One Forme, two ould Chaires, one Joynt stoole £1 10s

In the Kitchen: One Brewinge Pan, one Brewinge keeve, one great bras Pott, Fower small Brasse Pottes, three small Brasse Pannes, two Brasse kettels, one Brasse morter, Fower guns, two Dreppinge, a Payer of Anirons, two Spitts, Fower brandirons, one Saving Iron, one Fier Forke, one table-Board, one Chafing Dish £12

In the Dairy: Sixe Brass milch Panes, One tub, one Flesh tub and Clome £3; one Feild bed, Fower Bars of Iron, Hogsheds, tubs & Barrells, two skilletts £2.'

Upstairs this house had four chambers which were furnished as bedrooms with a total of six beds and three other small rooms and a loft which were used for storage. The parlour downstairs had an additional bed. In 1662 the house was assessed to be taxed on six hearths. Its fireplaces were in the three main downstairs rooms - parlour, hall and kitchen - and the three chambers over them. Two years later two of these fireplaces were recorded as being stopped up and almost certainly these were in the chambers over the hall and the kitchen because the one over the parlour was the most important. George Veale's six-hearth house in Gulval must have been fairly similar, with household goods worth a total of £64 compared with the £74 of Charles Ellis.

From the inventories studied very few houses in West Penwith were furnished on such a scale. John Adams lived in a one-hearth house in Sancreed, where he died in 1677. His household goods were then worth less than four pounds. They were listed as follows:

In the hall: 1 tableboard and form, 5 pewter dishes, 6 trenchers, 1 candlestick, 1 salt, 1 taster, 2 coules;

In the kitchen: 1 best pan, 1 tub, 1 coule, 1 vat, 6 wooden dishes, 1 chair, 2 brandirons, 1 best crock, spoons, 1 spinning turn;

In the Chamber: 2 beds, 2 coverlets, 2 pairs of sheets, 1 pair of blankets, clome vessels.'

These contents can be taken as a reasonable guide to the possessions of a typical middle-ranking household in West Penwith that was just prosperous enough to have an inventory taken, but they do raise a few puzzles. The Adams household was adequately provided with cooking and eating equipment and bedding, but appears to have had very little furniture: just one table, a bench, a chair and two mattresses, but no beds, cupboards or chests. Several reasons could explain the absence of such basic furniture from this inventory, but attempts to guess at them would not be helpful.

Analysis of sample inventories

A detailed analysis of twelve sample inventories from the three parishes of Gulval, Sancreed and Towednack gives a clearer picture of the main household possessions for those five in six families who had household goods valued at under £20. In most instances the valuations were reasonably reliable for second-hand possessions although they varied according to their condition and quality. Hence the description 'old' normally means worn or even battered. In making this analysis some arbitrary decisions were taken when several different items were lumped together under a single valuation, as happened with Charles Ellis's inventory.

Normally the deceaseds' beds and bedding accounted for between a third and two-fifths of their household goods (regardless of total value) and their cooking equipment for a similar proportion. Their other furniture and eating vessels were usually worth no more than a tenth to a fifth each of the total value of the household goods. From the tables opposite [or below] those with obvious deficiencies in particular categories include Thamsin Tripcony (A2) cooking, Nicholas Ginver (D3) eating, John Thomas (C1) other furniture as well as John Adams (A3) and Edward Dowing (B1) beds. Sometimes such anomalies can be explained by personal circumstances, such as old people living alone, or because some goods had been removed, bequeathed or just ignored.

This comparative analysis shows how much more detailed some inventories were than others and so enables us to understand better such rather vague entries as 'his bed furnished' or 'his pewter', especially when there is a valuation. In general, those with household goods of £10-19 (C & D) usually slept on feather mattresses, with finer sheets and larger and better bedsteads, although it is interesting to see that Widow Tripcony (A2) kept her feather mattress even though her cooking equipment was virtually worn out.

Only the very wealthy houses with more than £20 of household goods seem to have more than a very basic range of furniture in addition to their beds. All twelve in our sample below that level had one or more table-boards on a frame with a bench or two and perhaps a chair. Benches were probably so cheap that the appraisers of D2 & D3 did not bother to mention them, but stools were recorded for D1 & C3. Tablecloths were only found among categories C & D. The cupboards that were listed for everyone except A1 & A3 were a form of basic dresser or sideboard with open shelves for dishes, cups and so on. Virtually all houses had two or more chests for keeping clothes, but only A1 & D2 appear to have had a press, or what we would call a cupboard, for storing their clothes.

The most valuable cooking items were made of brass with the better equipped households having more, larger and more varied brass pans, pots and crocks. Cooking and preserving vessels made of iron or wood were much cheaper. The equipment for cooking on an open fire is listed in varying detail in these inventories and the process is well described by Iris Green in Chapter II on one-hearth houses. In this sample, all households ate from dishes and/or platters made of pewter, with the wealthier ones having more and larger ones. Silver spoons, brass candlesticks and items made of tin were only found among categories C & D, but everyone used a variety of wooden and earthenware vessels.

Some materials, such as horn, were so cheap that items made from them were rarely mentioned in these inventories. Thus we must not assume that any particular one gives a complete record of a household's possessions. However, when interpreted with care, these inventories do provide a wonderful insight into the common household objects and their uses in West Penwith more than three hundred years ago.

Detailed analysis of household goods in twelve sample inventories

Date	Parish		Status /occup	Inv. total £	H'hold goods £.s	bed £.s	Other furn £.s	cook £.s	eat £.s	other £.s	CRO refs
A1 1672	San	Mathew Skinner		14	3.00	1.10	8	1.00	3	-	S 1337
A2 1661	Gul	Thamsin Tripcony	widow	5	3.10	2.00	15	10	5	-	AP/T/851
A3 1677	San	John Adams		16	3.15	16	15	1.12	10	2	A 390/3
B1 1675	Gul	Edward Dowing		14	6.00	15	1.05	3.05	10	5	D 724.2
B2 1661	Gul	Richard Marten	fuller	26	6.10	3.10	13	2.00	10	-	M 821/1
B3 1678	Gul	Robert Ladner	b'smith	33	8.00	2.10	2.00	2.00	1.10	-	L 754/2
C1 1675	Gul	John Thomas	yeoman	56	11.02	2.05	12	4.10	15	3.00	AP/T/1140/2
C2 1669	Gul	Rich Donithorne	yeoman	100	12.15	4.05	1.00	3.10	2.15	1.05	D 658/2
C3 1661	Tow	William Russell		50	13.10	5.18	2.00	3.10	2.00	3	R 818/3
D1 1678	Tow	Jane Painter		100	17.10	6.05	2.07	6.16	1.16	6	P 1418/1
D2 1678	San	John Olivey	yeoman	144	18.10	7.10	1.02	7.05	2.10	3	O 247/2
D3 1674	Gul	Nicholas Ginver	yeoman	124	18.10	8.00	1.08	8.10	6	6	G 798/2

Beds & bedding
A1 30s. his bedding furnished;
A2 40s. bedstead, truckle bed, feather bed, 2 bolsters, pillow, 3 rugs, blanket, sheet, pair of sheets;
A3 16s. 2 beds, 2 coverlets, 2 pair of sheets, 1 pair of blankets;
B1 15s. 2 old bedsteads with bed clothes;
B2 70s. bedstead, fell bed, truckle bed, flock bed, 3 coverlets, 2 bolsters, pillow;
B3 50s. 2 beds and the clothing belonging to them;
C1 45s. half-headed bed, feather bed, feather bolster & pillow, pair of Dowlas sheets, pillow drawn, pair of blankets, 2 rugs, 2 old pairs(?) of canvas sheets;
C2 85s. 2 bedsteads, feather bed, bolster, 2 pillows, pair of blankets, coverlet, linen; bolster & bed clothes for serving boys;
C3 118s. the bed & bed clothes & feather beds & bolsters & pillowties;
D1 125s. 2 bedsteads, old truckle bed, 4 bolsters, 2 pillows, 6 old coverlets, old pair of Holland sheets, 3 pair of canvas sheets, 2 pillow drawers;
D2 150s. 4 feather beds furnished;
D3 160s. his bed furnished, 3 beds furnished;

Other furniture & soft furnishings
A1 8s. tableboard, frame & form, old press, 2 chests;
A2 15s. tableboard, frame & form, old frame, old cupboard, chest, old trunk;
A3 15s. tableboard & form, chair;
B1 25s. 3 tableboards & frames, form, chair, 2 old cupboards, 2 old chests;
B2 13s. tableboard, bench, 2 cupboards;
B3 40s. 2 tableboards, 2 forms, 3 small chairs, cupboard, 2 small chests;
C1 12s. tableboard & frame, small table & form, Dowlas board cloth;
C2 20s. tableboard, frame, form & bench, old cupboard, chest, 2 old coffers;
C3 40s. 2 tableboards & forms, cupboard, chair, stools, the coffers(?) & chests about the house, iron chest, carpet, board cloth;
D1 47s. old tableboard, form, 6 joined stools, 3 old cupboards, old sideboard, 3 old chests, 3 old board cloths & table napkins;

D2 22s. 2 table boards, chair, cupboard, press, 2 small chests, 2 carpets, 2 table cloths, 1 dozen table napkins;
D3 28s. 2 tableboards & frames, 2 old cupboards;

<u>Cooking & food preservation</u>

A1 20s. brass crock, scruff of brass, iron crock, posnet, old kettle, old tub, other timber vessels;
A2 10s. old brass, old timber vessels, brandiron;
A3 32s. best pan, best crock, tub, 3 cooles, vat, clome vessels, 2 brandirons;
B1 65s. 8 small brass pans, 2 old skillets, old frying pan, old iron pot, tub, coole;
B2 40s. old pan, 2 crocks, 4 old skillets, 2 old cues(?), flesh coole, standard, old pair of andirons, brandiron, old spit;
B3 40s. brass, 2 small iron crocks, old frying pan, timber vessels, small brandiron, griddle;
C1 90s. great pan, middle-sized pan, 2 old small pans, pan, big crock, great crock, 4 small crocks, skillet, iron cooler, 2 tubs, 3 vats, 2 bowls, 2 brandirons;
C2 70s. 3 brass pans, old pan, 2 brass crocks, 2 cooles, barrels, little keeve, little tub, 2 vats, bowle, 2 brandirons, gridiron;
C3 70s. 6 old brass pans, 3 old brass crocks, keeve barrels, tubs & hooped(?) vessels, andiron, brandirons, gridiron & spits;
D1 136s. 2 bigger pans, 4 small pans, brass crock, 2 small crocks, iron posnet, old keeves & tubs, 2 small kilderkins, old standard, salt barrel, old earthen vessels, old chathing? stove, old andirons, spit, firepan(?), prang(?);
D2 145s. 6 pans great & small, 3 brass crocks, iron crock, several wooden vessels, several earthen vessels, pair of andirons, 2 spits;
D3 170s. 5 brass pans, 3 brass pots, barrels, keeves & tubs, pair of andirons, 2 brandirons, spit;

<u>Eating</u>

A1 3s. 5 small pewter dishes, dishes, trenchers, spoons, a few old earthen vessels;
A2 5s. old pewter, spoon;
A3 10s. 5 pewter dishes, 6 wooden dishes, 6 trenchers, spoons, salt, taster(?);
B1 10s. 7 small pewter dishes, dishes, trenchers, spoons, 3 old jugs, clomen chafing dish;
B2 10s. 10 pewter dishes, 2 old saucers, old chafing dish;
B3 30s. pewter, clomen vessels;
C1 15s. 10 pewter platters, 3 saucers, dish, 3 platters;
C2 55s. silver cup, 3 silver spoons, 9 pewter platters, tin pint, tin salt, 8 clomen dishes, dishes, clome;
C3 40s. 4 silver spoons, 12 iron spoons, pewter dishes, podgers, saucers(?), cups & other pewter stuff, wooden dishes, trenchers & ladle boats(?), earthen vessels about the house;
D1 36s. 15 old platters, 6 podgers, 4 saucers, tin dish, 2 tin cups, 2 old flagons, old salt, 6 dishes, 6 spoons, chafing dish;
D2 50s. 12 silver spoons, 18 pewter dishes, maser dish, dishes, trenchers, spoons, chafing dish;
D3 6s. 6 pewter dishes;

<u>Others</u>

A2 2 old boards;
A3 2s. candlestick, spinning turn;
B1 5s. old pewter candlestick, great bible, old bucket, 4 old boards;
B2 old candlestick;
C1 60s. 2 old candlesticks, sword, basket & flaskets, several wash boards, pair of looms, 7 pair of slayes, little turn, other material for the looms, old wool turn, pair of wool cards, fuel;
C2 25s. brass candlestick, bucket, wool, loose cords, linen, cheese, butter, fuel;
C3 3s. 2 old brass candlesticks, books, old pounder(?);
D1 6s. brass candlestick, tin candlestick, old flasket & basket, old turn, old bucket, 2 old ladders;
D2 3s. 2 brass candlesticks, other candlestick, gun;
D3 6s. 1 brass candlestick, 2 spinning turns.

1 Reference - CRO E 244/2

V - ZENNOR AT THE TIME OF THE HEARTH TAX

JEAN NANKERVIS

What was Zennor like in 1664?

The parish was surprisingly similar to today. In 1664 forty-one heads of households paid tax for one (Plate 5) or more (Plate 3a and 3b) hearths. If one third of the inhabitants were too poor to be taxed that would make about sixty households in Zennor and a population around 260. Today's population is 182 electors and 63 children, making 245. There were about the same number of children in 1664 but the number of adults per household has fallen from 3.3 to 2.

The tax collectors of 1664 would have walked or ridden horseback along the paths from farm to farm. There was no wheeled traffic in Zennor in the 17th century and the road was used for droving not driving. The nineteen farms shown on the map are still here today but were divided into about 56 '£8 holdings'.[1] The prehistoric field patterns (Plate 2b) have changed very little since 1664.

Who were the people?

The Hearth Tax list was headed by the Vicar, Elizabeth Upcott and William Stevens who all paid for two hearths, then George Thomas who alone paid for three hearths in 1664. Altogether eleven paid for two hearths and the rest for one. The Eddy family was the wealthiest as farmers but three of them paid for only four hearths. Three of the two widows returned 'one short' in 1662 and were probably considered exempt until the rules were tightened in 1664.

ZENNOR INVENTORIES 1666 - 1704

Date	Name	Status	Hearths	Inv.Total	H'hold	Refs. in CRO
07/12/66	Thomas,G	yeo	3	30.37	7.87	AP/T 980
09/10/73	Robart,W	yeo	1	30.70	4.17	R 1037
Ja\F1674	Sweete,A	yo'swid	1	25.55	4.45	AP/S 1401
24/02/75	Perry ,J	yeo	1	24.07	1.95	P 1358
22/05/75	Michell,E-	-		23.75	4.80	M 1067
15/06/75	Thomas, J	hus-		31.58	nil	AP/T/1137
20/09/77	John,N	-		44.48	3.32	J 759
17/07/78	Upcott,E	widow	2	57.50	12.00	U 46
25/01/80	Roberts,H	widow-		64.06	14.43	R 1145
25/02/80	Berryman,A	yeo	2	18.45	11.98	B 1880
1680	Fowler,R	vicar	2	terrier	-	ARD/TER 44
05/04/83	Eddy,P	-		124.42	4.45	AP/E 387
11/03/82	Maddern,F	-	1	42.45	3.10	M/1191
11/30/82	Tregurtha,T	yeo	-	15.50	4.00	T/1281
04/07/83	Thomas,W	yeo	1	239.35	6.75	AP/T 1301
17/11/85	Porthmear,A	tinner	-	25.92	2.50	P 1636
24/04/88	Thomas,O	widow	-	101.30	5.15	AP/ T 1401
03/11/90	UdyJ,Elder	yeo	1	140.50	9.00	AP/E 458
08/10/90	EddyJ,yr	yeo	1	164.45	3.50	AP/E 435
13/12/92	Stevens,E	yeo	1	29.30	4.20	AP/S 1913
14/11/97	Phillip, R	yeo	-	61.15	5.50	P 2228
01/12/97	Phillip, F	yeo	1	55.67	11.67	P/2224
13/11/04	Quick,J	yeo	1	86.80	4.75	AP/Q 41

new style dates used   decimal currency

SCYTHE

The ones too poor to be taxed were agricultural labourers, tinners and those who partly relied on charity. In 1641 all men over 18 were listed on the Protestation Return and in Zennor there were 83 with 43 different surnames. Only 31 surnames are given in 1664 which is 12 less. Some men did not return from the Civil War and some families may have moved or died out. The seven empty houses listed on the Hearth Tax Return show this decline in population.

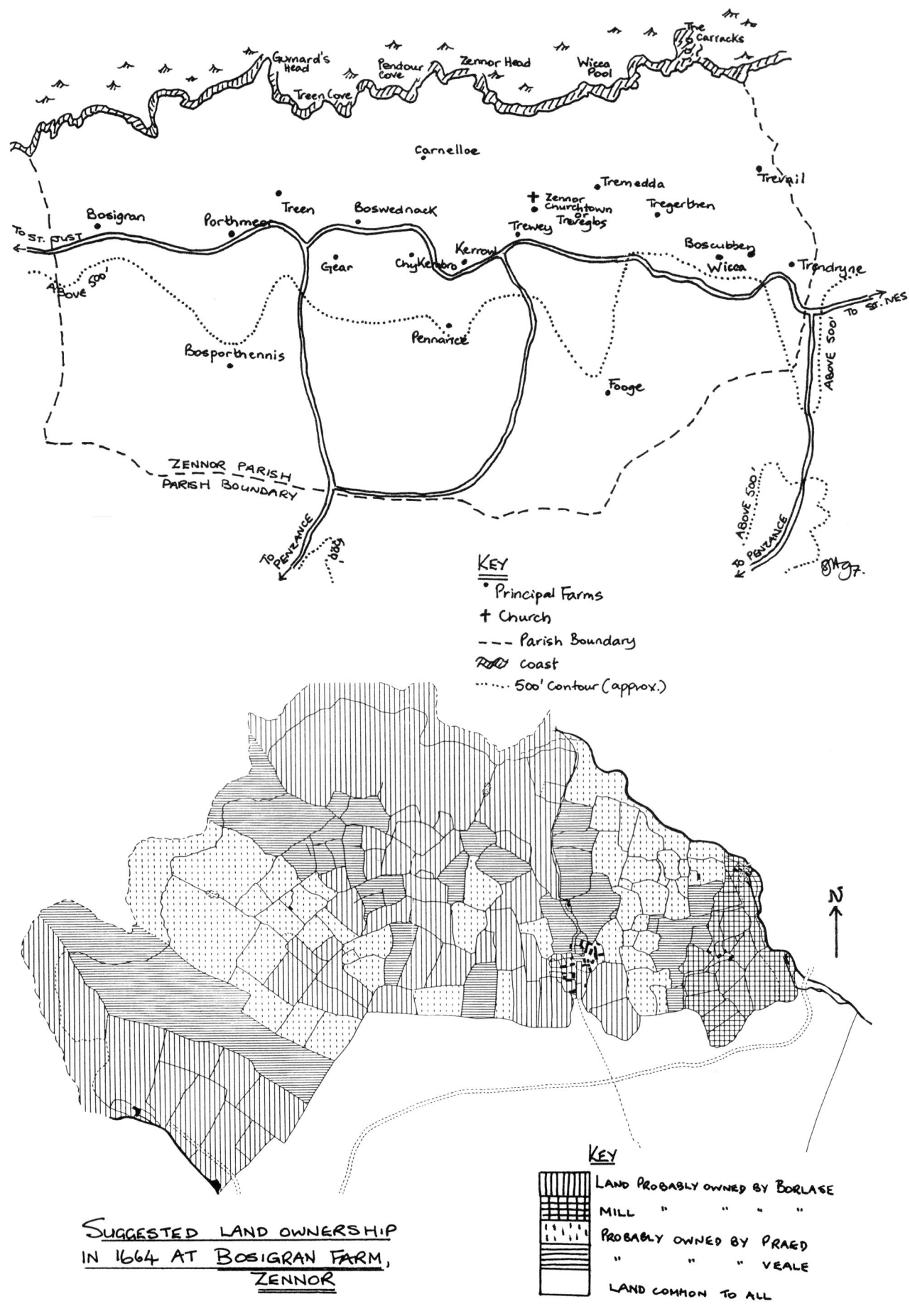

What can we find out about the people and where they lived in Zennor?

To find out who lived where I have studied probate and other records both before and after the reign of Charles II. It was disappointing to find only eight places and a mill mentioned but the terrier of 1680 describes the vicarage. With 22 inventories and 14 wills we get a tantalising glimpse of 16 families.

THOMAS. George Thomas alias Truthwall headed a large and prosperous family but by the time he died he must have passed on much of his wealth to his six children. He owned a sword, musket and bandoleer and these weapons show he was a man of status. He had 'kievs, barrels, dishes, ladle with suchlike decayed timber in his work', and 2 ladders. 'His work' usually means mining work. He was probably living at Treen in Zennor where mining was first recorded in 1596. He had a well furnished house (for Zennor), six silver spoons and a mazer dish. He left two of his sons, William and James £5 or 1s each if they did not agree!

James Thomas died in 1675 and had no household goods so was probably a bachelor living with his brother William who was married but childless. He left his property to his brothers and sister, also to his sister-in-law - 'To Sible Thomas my half of the cow that is betwixt us. To brother Matthew's daughter Jane the half heifer that is betwixt us'. William, the other brother told not to quarrel, was taxed on only one hearth but when he died his inventory was the highest in Zennor. His total assets included a lease for Boswednack £24, one for Treen £15 and £2 for one at scanty Bosprennis. He had £145 invested, most on specialties, two brass pans and two brass crocks. Crocks were probably bigger than pans and used for brewing, in the dairy and for cooking. William's widow Orchard Thomas left everything to her sister Tamsin Maddern and Tamsin's children Matthew, John, Martin and Elizabeth. 'To Elizabeth wife of John Berriman £5 also the house on the north side and garden, part of my Tenement in Boswednack and one cow's grass to pasture and commons for pigs and sheep.' This implies Orchard had more than one house at Boswednack and her total inventory was the fifth highest in Zennor so she was a wealthy widow.

UDY, EDY OR EDDY. In 1664 Udy was an old spelling for Edy, later Eddy. The family lived at Bosigran and their inventories were the next highest in Zennor. The one for John Eddy the Younger lists a hall, higher house and lower house. This means his home was three rooms, built in a line with a hearth in the hall. It is surprising that this comparatively rich family lived in a house that was single storey. John Eddy the Elder had a butter house with six brass pans valued at £5. In his hall were 10 plates, no doubt on the cupboard, a bed, chair and a great chest which totalled £2. In his kitchen were crocks, table-board, bed and other small things worth £2. Again this implies a single storey house but may have had hearths in the kitchen and hall. From John the Elder's will we gain a tiny glimpse of his family. His wife Jane and father David were to receive their 'maintenance of meat and drink and apparel with houseroom, washing and attendance and all things that may be convenient' during their lives. His eldest son David was to look after his brother John until he came of age, having his labour.

MAZOR DISH - A POLISHED WOODEN BOWL

BERRYMAN. Bosigran, the westernmost farm in Zennor, was in four parts including a mill on Porthmear river which flowed down from Bosprennis. Over the next two centuries the Eddys spread throughout the parish and the last one left Zennor in the 1940s. In 1692 their neighbours the Berrymans had a lease on part of Porthmear[2] which was a three farm hamlet. The Berrymans still farm in the parish today as do the Osbornes who appeared in Zennor for the first time on the Hearth Tax list.

In 1679 Arthur Berryman's son William inherited a tenement at Treen from his father and paid John Nance £50 for the lease. Leases were often renewed from one generation to the next. Treen, being one of the bigger farm hamlets in Zennor, was divided in five but all the farmers that mention it in documents also leased other land. Arthur Berryman's inventory is surprisingly low but his bees were valued at £1, twice as much as Orchard Thomas's four stocks for 10s. Arthur and his brother Nicholas Berryman senior, paid for two hearths each and this branch of the family settled at Porthmear. Their cousin Nicholas Berryman junior was a member of the Churchtown line.

Simplified BERRYMAN Family Tree

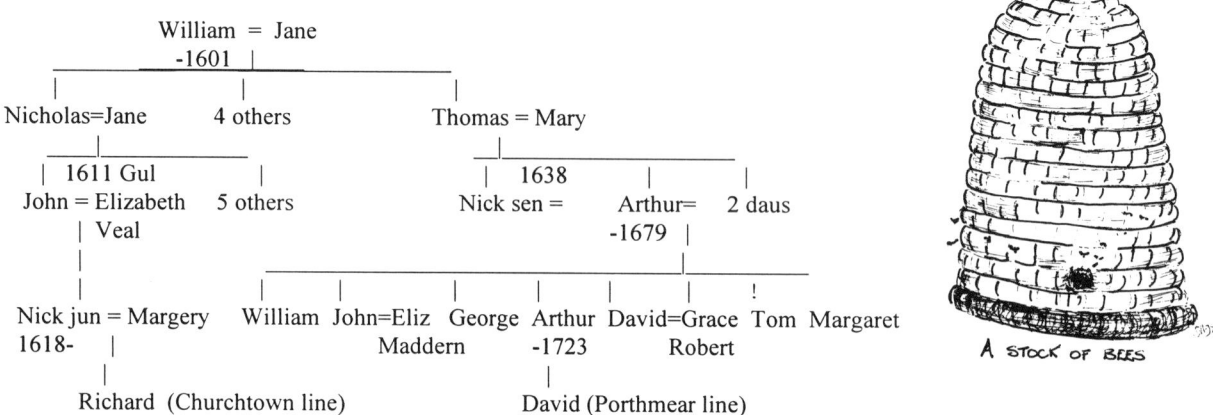

A STOCK OF BEES

```
                    William = Jane
                      -1601  |
         _____|_____
         |              |                       |
   Nicholas=Jane    4 others              Thomas = Mary
         |                                       |
      ___|_____                     _____|_____
      | 1611 Gul       |                    | 1638   |              |
    John = Elizabeth  5 others           Nick sen = Arthur=      2 daus
      |   Veal                                      -1679 |
      |                          _____|_____
      |                          |        |       |      |        |       |
   Nick jun = Margery         William  John=Eliz George Arthur David=Grace Tom Margaret
   1618-   |                           Maddern         -1723  Robert
           |                                                  |
       Richard (Churchtown line)                        David (Porthmear line)
```

MADDERN. John and Matthew Maddern had a lease on one of the tenements at Porthmear in 1688. Perhaps Francis Maddern was their uncle who died in 1682 leaving a lease at Treen worth £20. He was the only person in Zennor with barley, 8 bushels in March. The Cornish bushel held 24 gallons, being three times bigger than the English. If the barley was in sheaves it would have been fed to livestock, or if in grains kept for seed, but such a large quantity on March 11th suggests he was a brewer.

PERRY. Walking eastward from Treen the next farm is Boswednack which was divided into four holdings. Here John Perry died in 1675 and left his part to his wife Jone during her life and then to his son George. The value of his inventory is not high but included a spinning turn. The family was first mentioned in Zennor in 1507, when Thomas Perry had a tin works.

PHILLIPS. Their neighbours at Boswednack were probably the Phillips who fought on both sides during the Civil Wars. Was this a family with divided loyalties? The Phillips brothers John, James and Thomas, farmed two parts of Boswednack and had another lease at Trewey. In 1642 Thomas Phillips, the youngest, was 'pressed for the wars in the King's Majesty's service' and died three years later. James died the next summer and may have been the constable who joined a local rising against the king and was hanged for it. James's widow Alice had two children at home and in 1664 was living in a house with one hearth. John, the eldest brother, died before 1662 leaving a son Francis. Although Francis was taxed on one hearth he lived in one of the better houses in Zennor. It was unusual to have as many as three beds and valued at £4.15.0. He was aged about 70 when he made his will and left his daughter Jone [Joan] '40s provided she goes from me to live'! Was this an unhappy family and was there a sense of foreboding?

Robert, Francis's second son, made his will in September and was buried six weeks later followed soon after by his father's death. Robert's house was one of the few that had two storeys. As well as a hall and milkhouse it had a kitchen with a bed in it and a chamber upstairs. His eldest son Gabriel, only eleven years old, was to maintain the four younger children until they could 'get their living'. If his wife Margaret married again, Gabriel would inherit the lease of Bosprennis worth £40 and was to pay her 40 shillings a year. Probate was granted in 1697 and next year widow Margaret wed Thomas Renowden.

ROBERTS. William Roberts junior was taxed for one hearth and may be the blacksmith mentioned in Alice Sweete's probate documents. He died in 1673, his possessions were good quality and as a farmer he was the seventh richest in Zennor. His widow Honour died six years later leaving her lease on Chykembro to her sons John and William who were still under age. Her daughter Grace married David Berryman. One of the overseers of her will was her sister's husband James Quick.

QUICK. James Quick wed Jane Knight alias Roberts in 1649 and the Knight/Roberts family appear in the records with one or both surnames. Also in 1649 William Knight junior, wed Honour Chekembra alias Williams. He is probably the William Roberts junior above. Marriages were often between neighbours, hence the paucity of surnames. The Quicks were a leading family in the area and often acted as assessors for Zennor inventories. Only Nicholas Berryman appeared more often in this capacity but John Thomas was another regular and so were the Michells. The goods of the deceased were usually appraised by the eldest son or a member of the family with one of the chief men of the parish.

James Quick died in 1703 leaving two tenements on Mill Downs above Trewey, but of course, he might have been anywhere in Zennor in 1664 when he was taxed for one hearth. His will gives a fascinating glimpse of the family. He left his wife £10 a year and £50 to the person she named at her decease. We can just imagine the family crowding around with favours in the hope Jane would name them as she breathed her last! The household goods were to be divided into three and Jane had one third by lot.

MICHELL. Edward Michell died in March 1674/5 and by word of mouth left all to his mother Sybill. Edward's inventory lists good quality possessions, particularly clothes and, where many name only one bed, he had a bed and truckle bed. He had no farming interests but owned a fulling gown. The Michells were usually found in the Churchtown area so was his 'One small tenement on 2 lives for £6' near Zennor river?

PORTHMEAR. Anthony Porthmear died 1685 and was the only one described as a tinner. Although there were others it was not their main occupation, for example James Udy was described as 'tynner' when he renewed a lease for Bosigran mill in 1687. Five Porthmears were on the Protestation Return but none on the Hearth Tax list. Perhaps they were too poor as Anthony's house was sparsely furnished with only a bed, 'cubards' and a table board. In 1642 a tenement at Trewey was known as Thomas Pormeare's so this might be the 'One chattel leas £3' Anthony left.

SWEETE. Mrs. Alice Sweete was a widow and 'Mrs.' shows she was a person of some standing. Sam Sweete was the immediate past vicar of Zennor. She left 'Land on one old life now in being in Zennor Churchtown £5'. If this was for a fifth of Churchtown she had the same amount of land as the vicar. Richard FOWLER was the incumbent and taxed on two hearths but died in 1669. Anthony Rondell was vicar in 1680 when he described the two storey house. The glebe was between six and ten acres scattered throughout the Churchtown land being one fifth of Treveglos Farm. As well as this tillable land the commons on the Downs and cliff for pasture and fuel were shared between the five holdings. In 1727 the vicar said a grist mill paid him 3s a year.

TREGURTHA. When Thomas Tregurtha died in 1682 he had a lease on 'a little grist mill for one life

'£9', probably on Zennor river. James Eddy was working Bosigran mill in 1687 and William Stevens had the lease of Trevail mill in 1715. Tregurtha was not listed for the hearth tax and his inventory is the lowest for this period. He owned one small cow and four goats which probably grazed the commons.

UPCOTT. Elizabeth Upcott, born a Veale, came from a landowning family in Gulval. She married John Berryman in 1611 and their son was Nicholas Berryman junior. Her second husband also pre-deceased her and she sounds a grand old lady aged about 90 when she died in 1678. She had no interests in farming but owned a moiety of a house in Penzance. Among other things she left her son '1 cupboard now in the middle chamber', to his daughter Margery a brass pan about 5 gallons, and to her daughter Jane Donithorne 'one chest at the stairs head where I live'. Thus, her house had two hearths, a middle chamber and stairs. Chambers were usually upstairs and a middle room implies one on either side. There are only three surviving 17th century houses in Zennor that were two storey.[3] The vicarage had two rooms upstairs, Wicca Farm House (Plate 2a) was much too big but Tregarthen had three chambers so she probably lived there in some importance.

FIVE GALLON BRASS POT

JOHN. Nicholas John might have lived at Trevail on the eastern border of the parish and a mining area. He had an adventure in tin works worth £1, and wool worth 3s. He was one of the wealthier farmers and his goods were valued above average. Cows were usually worth about £2 but his were £2.10s.0d. each. Even this did not equal his neighbour Edward Stevens who had a prize ox worth £3.5s.0d.

STEVENS. William, John and Edward Stevens were on the Protestation Return of 1641 and in 1662 William headed the family with three hearths. Wicca (Plate 2a) had three fireplaces so this could have been their home. In 1664 William's son Job was paying for one of the three. Edward paid for one hearth, possibly at Trevail mill where his son William had the lease in 1715. Edward's inventory included an adze, a lathe and three old sacks so he worked with wood.

WICCA AS IT MAY HAVE LOOKED BY THE LATE 17th

Edward left his son William '4 milk cows, 2 oxen and 2 of my best horses and 4 sheep and all my corn and money and half my household goods and my badon.' The badon was probably a gun belt and indicates his social standing. Edward's inventory was taken four weeks after his death and does not include these possessions. During this month William took his inheritance and wed Zenobia, daughter of James Quick of Mill Downs.

What was farming like in Zennor?
Zennor was, and still is, essentially a farming community. In 1664 parishioners kept cattle, sheep, pigs and poultry, they produced butter, cheese, beef and honey. The average farmer in Zennor had £2.39 invested in corn and £18.79 in livestock. All had cattle, most had pigs, sheep, a mare, a nag and a colt. Of the poorest even Perry the spinner had a mare and Maddern the brewer a nag.

The figures below [4] show Zennor had about 20% more in cattle and 20% less in corn than the average for Penwith in 1680. The fields in Zennor are very rocky and corn takes a long time to ripen on the north coast making the parish more suitable for pasture farming.

% of investment in Penwith and Zennor

	1620	1680	Zennor
cattle	42	44	61.5
horses	14	19	16.5
corn	25	28	10.5
sheep	17	8	8.0
pigs	2	3	2.0
implements			1.5

AN UNCARVED WOODEN CHEST

It seems Bosigran was the only farm run exclusively by one family. The fields on the plain were in a patchwork pattern (Plate 1b) surrounded by undivided commons [see map]. In 1662 John Borlase, gent, of Pendeen (Plate 4), bought part of Bosigran. Veale and Praed owned about a third each. John Eddy the Elder left leases for half of higher and half of lower Bosigran while John Eddy the Younger had the other halves. John the Elder owned 20 sheep and lambs, 15 goats and kids, 10 small pigs, 4 cows and 7 young bullocks, 3 calves and 4 small oxen, 2 nags, a mare and 4 colts. John the Younger had a half share of three steers but owned a red steer and one with a white star. As it was only October he still had 19s worth of cheese and butter in the house. Sheep and goats milk was made into cheese and we can imagine their goats on The Galvers. Perhaps Carn Galver is a corruption of *gavar* which is the Cornish word for goat. Philip Eddy kept geese, ducks and hens in his yard. As he died in April he had no corn, only 4 pigs at the end of the winter and no colts as none were born yet for the year. When Borlase granted David Eddy a lease in 1714 it gave him the right to make dung in the townplace![5] The Eddys owned two of the four bulls in Zennor and their investment in livestock was well above the parish average of £18.16s.0d.

FARMING INTERESTS FROM ZENNOR INVENTORIES

	Total	Cattle	Sp/gts	Pgs/Py	Horses	Corn	Imps
J.Udy, elder	46.50	25.00	3.00	1.50	9.00	7.00 mow	1.00
J. Eddy, yr	44.50	23.50	2.50	1.50	9.50	6.00 mow	0.50
P.Eddy	38.77	28.40	4.16	0.58	5.30		0.20
W.Thomas	43.65	30.00	4.00	0.15	2.75	3.00 m/f	0.50
F.Phillip	29.00	15.50	-	0.75	8.50	2.75 mow	1.50
J.Quick	28.80	21.50	1.50	0.50	3.00	2.00 mow	0.30
W.Robart	25.47	17.50	1.50	0.52	2.50	2.16	0.21
N. John	25.20	10.75	2.50	0.60	6.00	4.00 field	0.35
E.Stevens	22.40	13.75	5.00	0.15	3.50	-	-
G.Thomas	20.25	8.00	1.50	-	-	10.00 mow	0.75
J.Thomas	19.42	18.66	0.75	-	-	-	-
A.Porthmear	17.42	10.00	1.12	0.30	5.00	1.00	-
R.Phillip, elder	14.10	1.40	0.45	0.55	8.50	3.00 mow	0.50
A.Sweete	14.00	12.50	-	-	1.50 field		-
F.Maddern	8.80	6.50	2.50	0.25	2.50	2.00	-
A.Berryman	5.47	1.50	3.00	0.22	-	1.00	-
J. Perry	3.33	0.50	0.57	0.76	-	1.50	-
T.Tregurtha	2.00	2.00	-	-	-	-	-
O.Thomas	2.00	1.50	-	-	-	-	-

Decimal currency. m/f =in mowhay and field, mow=mowhay, sp/gt=sheep and goats, pg/py=pigs and poultry.

When William Thomas died his eight cows were in full milk and he had a rack of cheeses valued at 5/- with three deal boards. His inventory was taken on July 4th when his corn was in the fields as well as his mowhay. 1683 must have been an exceptional year as wheat does not usually ripen that early for cutting. In 1677 Nicholas John still had all his corn in the field in September. Corn was very scarce in the winter of 1673/4 when Alice Sweete died so perhaps bad weather contributed to her death.

FIVE POUND CHEESES ON A DEAL BOARD

33

James Quick was one of the top cattle owners in the parish producing milk and beef. Bullocks were fattened for 3-4 years and the average farmer in Zennor had four, so beef production was important. Oxen, sometimes described as draught bullocks, were later killed for beef. Throughout Zennor they were used for ploughing. Edward Stevens' 28 sheep were valued at 3s.6d. each and may have been an improved breed as the usual price was 3s.

Although farming in Zennor was growing for the expanding markets at the end of the 17th century, the parish population had yet to recover from the Civil War.

BIDDICK - A LONG-BLADED TURF DIGGER OFTEN APPEARING IN INVENTORIES. ALSO KNOWN AS A BEATAX

Refs
1. Tythe book for Zennor in CRO DDX/110/23
2. Three Hundred Years on Penwith Farms, Penwith Local History Group, 1994
3. Statutory List of Buildings of Historic Interest in Zennor 1988
4. Cornwall in the 17th Century, James Whetter, Lodenek Press 1974
5. CAU reports for the National Trust (unpublished) 1987 particularly for Bosigran

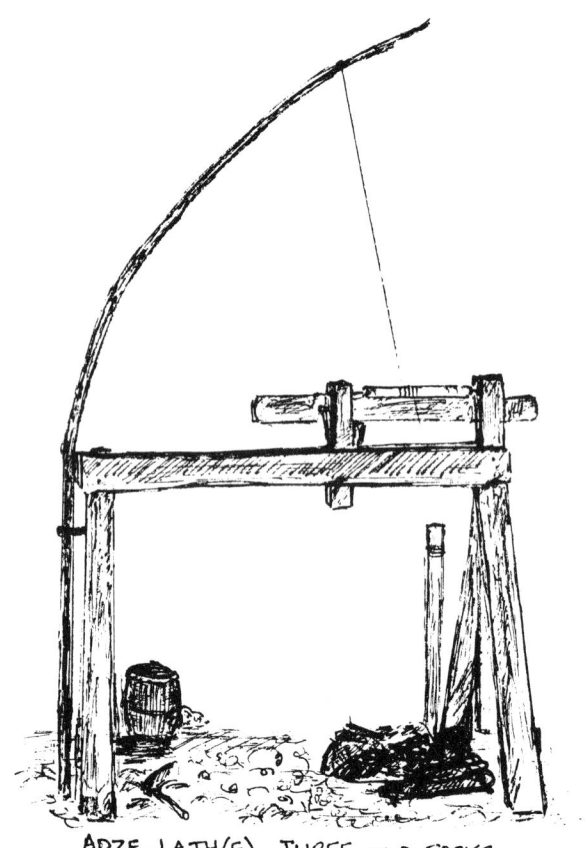

ADZE, LATH(E), THREE OLD SACKS....

VI. WEST PENWITH SHEEP: WHERE DID THEY COME FROM, WHEN WERE THEY BROUGHT HERE, WHAT WERE THEY USED FOR?

HELEN BEAUFORT-MURPHY

By the mid 17th century more than 2000 generations of domestic sheep had grazed the windswept, hilly pastures of West Penwith for over 5000 years. Consequently, Cornwall's sheep played a major part in the development of the Cornish economy and the evolution of British sheep. Articles related to spinning and weaving often appear in 17th Century wills and inventories. According to Carew's survey of the county, in 1602 nearly every household had at least a few sheep and many of the larger farms had good sized flocks;[4] so there were many sheep in 17th century Cornwall.

Sheep and goats were man's first domesticated farm animals.[6,10] Man had domesticated wild Asiatic Mouflon sheep and Bezzoar goats and was cultivating wheat and barley in the Near and Far East by 9000BC, followed by cattle and pigs several thousand years later.[6] Wild Mouflon sheep, an ancestor of domestic sheep,[6,17] have small, slender bodies and long legs and both sexes have horns. They are brown with a white under-belly, and a self-shedding fleece consisting of an outer coat of short, bristly hairs (or kemp) with a shorter, woolly under coat.[17] The feral Soay sheep currently living on the Island of Soay, of the St. Kilday group of islands, are similar to the wild Mouflon.[2]

Neolithic Period 5000-2000BC. West Penwith's first farmers were the Neolithic settlers who arrived here around 4000BC bringing Cornwall's first domesticated sheep with them.[5,20] They also built the massive megalithic Portal Dolmens (such as Chun Quoit near Morvah), the remains of which still dominate the Penwith landscape.[5,20] The sheep were similar to their wild Mouflon ancestors (Plate 1a) with self-shedding, coarse hairy fleeces. The skins were used to make clothing and covers for the door-ways for their houses.[14] Awls used to make holes in animal skins, and skin scrapers, were used by 3400BC,[17] but no evidence has been found of textile production for that period. Archaeological evidence shows that by 3000BC peat bogs were forming on previously forested uplands as a result of the Neolithic land clearing and farming.[6]

NEOLITHIC SHEEP AND CHÛN QUOIT

BRONZE AGE

Bronze Age (2000 to 1000BC). Bronze Age sheep were the same brown colour as the wild Mouflon ancestor, but the outer hair had become finer with fewer coarse kempy hairs and the under wool was both finer and longer than that of the Neolithic Age sheep. The ratio of domestic animals in Britain at this time was around 76% sheep, 14% cattle, 4% pigs and 4% horses. Wheeled carts were in use in some parts of the country.[17]

Iron Age (1000 to 43AD). Sheep were the most numerous domestic animal in Cornwall and the majority of them still had self-shedding fleeces. Archaeological remains of the complete bodies of 68 sheep, 18 pigs, 14 cattle, but no horses, were identified from The Rumps, an Iron Age, Fortified Hillfort and Village on a coastal headland near Newquay.[17] Spindles and whorls for spinning yarn, as well as loom weights, and bone combs of the type used for preparing wool for weaving (from the same period), were also

HAND SPINDLE AND WHORL

found at The Rumps and other locations in Britain, so textile production was becoming wide-spread.[17] Sheep with continuously growing, non-moulting hair appeared by 2000BC but this type of sheep had to be clipped and the tensile strength of iron was needed to make clippers large enough to clip sheep wool.[17] Therefore, until the development of iron, sheep with continuously growing wool would not have been very desirable. Continued selection for improved quality had gradually produced fleeces in which the coarse kemp hairs were replaced with softer, finer hair, while the underwool increased in length and fineness. Sheep with fleeces of various shades of grey, black and an occasional solid white, as well as the original brown shades were common. Besides the variety of colours Iron Age sheep had shorter legs and longer, softer fleeces than those of the Bronze Age and were more similar in size and appearance to the Shetland and Orkney sheep of today than those of the Neolithic period.[17]

Sheep on Penwith manors in the Domesday Book of 1086. The Domesday Survey lists a total of 1,342 sheep, 124 cattle, 169 horses, and 43 pigs among 15 manors of Penwith, demonstrating that the number of sheep in Penwith was greater than all the other types of livestock put together. Meanwhile, the long woolled breeds imported into Britain by the Romans contributed to the gradual improvement of British sheep.[17]

Shepherds were a vitally important part of British sheep and wool production as indicated by the 11th century Right of the Shepherd (Rectitudines Singularum Personarum). This gave a shepherd the right to keep some of his own sheep with the Lord's; to fold the manorial flock on his own land for 12 nights in mid-winter (for manure); to take 1 lamb and 1 fleece of the year's crop, or the milk of 2 Ewes on every Sunday; to have the milk of the flock 7 nights after the Spring Equinox; and to have a daily bowl of whey or buttermilk all summer.[17]

Crimes tried at the Sheriff's Tourns (a bi-annual session of the hundred court to try the cases of people accused of crimes in a given area) emphasize the historical importance of sheep in the economy of West Penwith. For instance, the Assize roles of 1284 relating to the Hundred of Penwith included 10 murders and 2 instances of sheep stealing, while in 1302 crimes included 4 murders, and 1 case of sheep and oxen stealing by one Lawrence of Penzance and his son John (a vagrant).[15]

Between 1350 and 1550 England changed from being the main supplier of raw wool in Europe to being the leading manufacturer of woollen cloth. Britain grew the most and best wool in Europe and charged 33% tax on exporting raw wool to discourage the export of wool and encourage British cloth production.[17]

FISHING NETS AND BASKET, MAGLAN, HOOKS AND NET NEEDLE

Sheep in 17th century Penwith: There were 3 sheep for every 1 human in Britain at the beginning of the 16th century as the result of peasant bondage and forced labour on manorial land in the past.[10] However, by the 17th century British farming had changed completely, from the subsistence level of the peasant to the commercial level of the yeoman farmer who earned his living from the soil and had some control over his land.[21] An example of this new life style was Yeoman Thomas Coell, who was a relatively wealthy farmer/fisherman of St. Goran.[21] The inventory of his chattlel possessions (valued at £125) illustrate his wide range of activities. It included 25 sheep, 3 horses, 3 cattle, 5 pigs, poultry, a saw, 2 spinning wheels, wool cards and 9 pounds of wool, as well as a fishing boat, a seine and a large variety of fishing equipment.

In his 1602 Survey of Cornwall Carew[4] stated that, fortunately, the small bodied ancient breed of Cornish Hayre sheep were seldom seen anymore. Cornish Hayre sheep were descendants of Iron Age sheep and by the 17th century were usually in poor health due to bad land management practices and liver disease (now known to be caused by liver flukes carried by snails). In addition, they produced poor quality fleeces (2-3pounds) of short, coarse grey wool. However, he noted with pleasure that the pastures were much improved since being enclosed and manured. He also mentioned that many Cornish sheep were of the newer breeds with large bodies and long, fine woolled fleeces without any kempy hairs, that compared with (if not surpassed) the eastern flocks, in health, fineness of wool, lambing, milk production and meat flavour. The sheep to which Carew referred may have been of an early long-wooled-type imported from Spain at the end of the 16th century.[17] The majority of these sheep were solid white, and were probably similar in body and fleece type to today's medium woolled Romney Sheep.[2]

The quality of fleece and body conformation continued to improve and by the mid 17th century the bi-products of sheep were also exploited as an important part of the economy.[17] Milk was the most important economic bi-product in the 17th century followed, in order of importance, by wool, manure, guts, and skin of the animals. On the other hand, sheep meat did not become economically important until towns started to expand after the beginning of the 18th century.[17]

Sheep milk was used for making cheese. The women did all the sheep milking and cheese making, and they kept half of the whey or buttermilk.[17]

Wool. In the 17th century `clipping' referred to cutting the fleece from a sheep, and `shearing' referred to harvesting the grain from the field. 'Two faire days followed by 1 faire week' was needed in mid June for the annual sheep clipping. This allowed time for the sheep to dry after washing, the as well as clipping, the sheep to become hardened to the cold and for the new wool to `rise' sufficiently to protect them from bad weather. If it rained during the fortnight following the clipping the sheep were brought back from the pasture and kept in the fold for protection.[17]

Sheep clipping in 17th century Cornwall was a major annual event of social and economic importance that would have been eagerly looked forward to by all concerned. Wealthy land owners often hired a piper to provide entertainment in the evening for everyone involved with the clipping. Clipping could involve most of the inhabitants of a given area, from the children to the elderly, as well as outsiders who came to assist with the occasion.[22] For instance, William Thomas (Zennor) was one of a large family who probably all helped with the sheep clipping; and when he died in July 1683 he had 23 fleeces worth £1 (Chapter V). Each shepherd received the fleece of his `bellwether'.[17] A wether is a castrated adult male sheep, a bellwhether is one that wears a bell and is trained to lead the flock and answer to its name.

Each clipper provided 2 pairs of clipping shears, and a whetstone was shared between 2 clippers. An average clipper could clip 3 and a half score of sheep a day, but a really good one could clip 4 and a half score. A clipper was paid 4d for each score of sheep, plus ale, bread and cheese at mid-day and roast mutton at night. It took 2 fleece winders to keep up with the fleeces of every 5 clippers. Each fleece was rolled up individually and tied with the neck wool (as it is today). While the clipping was in progress children collected the scattered locks of wool, the best of which were rolled up with the fleeces, and the poor quality pieces put into baskets and given to the poor.[17]

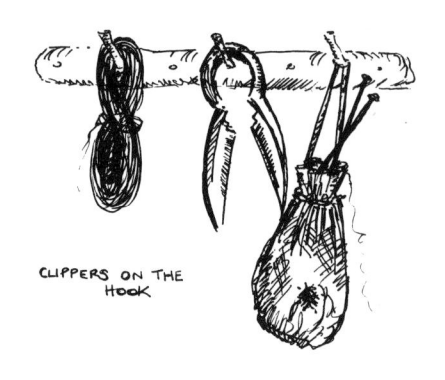

CLIPPERS ON THE HOOK

Wool buyers paid the highest prices for clean wool so the fleeces were placed on raised boards in the barn, to keep them clean and dry. One wonders if William Thomas (above) kept his 23 fleeces securely locked in the barn until they were sold because, according to Carew,[4] prudent farmers did so to protect their fleeces from 'theevish servants'? The buyers weighed the raw wool in stones (14 pounds) and bought it in `1 tod lots' (28 pounds).[17]

Sheep were greased for scab and lice once a year in mid October. The greasing was done, staple by staple, with a mixture of melted tallow and tar that was developed by Best (a Yorkshire sheep farmer) in the 17th century and it took 2 people to do 7 sheep a day.[17]

CLIPPING

The production of woollen cloth.[1,8,16] Cornish clothiers, who were usually yeoman farmers (such as Thomas Coell of St. Goran[21]), produced the hand woven cloth from raw wool in their own homes. It was a highly organized affair that could involve an entire family as well as numerous additional helpers. The raw wool was washed, scoured, dyed and dried; after which it was carded by children. Spinning was women's work, even though the turn (or spinning wheel) would have (usually) been owned by the man of the house. An example of this is demonstrated by the will of John Michell of Zennor in 1675 when a turn was left to his wife Jone. (Chapter V). An experienced spinner could spin a pound of wool into yarn in a day, and it took about 5 carders to keep up with a spinner. It also took an average of 5 experienced spinners to supply the daily needs of a weaver. Until the middle of the 16th century spinning was done on a spinning wheel known as the Great Wheel, which was turned by hand by the spinner who stood at its side and walked back and forth several steps with each turn of the wheel.[1] Any of the women who did the spinning for John Perry of Zennor[11] would have walked about 30 miles a day. In the mid 16th century the smaller, faster, treadle driven `Saxony Wheel' was developed and became popular in parts of Britain. However, the Great Wheel was the one most commonly used in 17th century Cornwall.

CHILDREN CARDING.

THE 'GREAT' SPINNING WHEEL

A clothier wove the cloth on a loom in his home. A bolt of cloth was about 34 inches wide, but it could not be more than 18 yards long because of the capacity of the warping board used to wind the warp threads. (The bolts of Harris Tweed produced by the highly skilled craftsmen on the Herbrides Islands today still involve the same basic procedures but their finished bolts of cloth can be up to 85 yards long). A warping board is a series of pegs inserted into boards on a wall in a specific pattern, over which the warp threads are wound in readiness for the weaver to put on his loom. When a bolt of cloth was taken off the loom it underwent the 'fulling process' that involved washing and milling to remove the dirt, raise the nap and shrink the cloth. Before the invention of the fulling-mill the process was done by fullers who walked up and down on the cloth in a stream or large tank of water[7]. Edward Michell was a fuller with a small tenement near Zennor River (chapter V). When the cloth was dry the nap on the surface of the material was brushed with teasels and sheared to a uniform height. Then the material was folded in half (lengthwise) and rolled into a bolt for market. Depending on the weather, the entire process took about a week.[17] The weavers of Sennen (such as those of the Sennen hamlet of Escalls) were famous for the quality of their work. Their cloth, known as 'the best in the west', was taken by pack horse to Penzance to sell.[9]

Manure: Sheep manure was third in economic importance after sheep milk and wool. It was carefully collected from the sheep folds and sold as fertilizer. In addition, sheep were rented out to other farmers, for specific periods, to fertilize the newly harvested grain fields. In which case a sheep farmer was paid for the use of his flock as mobile fertilizers, and he got the use of the grain stubble as forage for his animals.[17]

Gut bi-products: Sheep stomachs were treated and made into containers to hold liquids and 'bags' for bag pipes throughout the British Isles and probably included the Cornish form of Bag Pipes. 'Catgut,' despite old stories to the contrary, was made from the guts of sheep not cats! The gut of sheep was treated and made into strings and bows for a wide variety of musical instruments, such as harps.[17]

WEAVING

Skin bi-products: Sheep skins were used for making clothing, footwear, and bags to carry things in, just as the Neolithic settlers had done in the past.[14] In addition, both sheep and lamb skins were made into high quality vellum (parchment) that was used instead of paper on which to write formal, legal documents. Vellum is not made by a tanning process in the way that leather is. Instead, the hair is loosened from the skin by soaking in an alkaline solution (such as lime) and rinsed. The wet skin is then put on a stretcher and scraped with a blunt knife to remove the hair, dried, and polished with pumice. Sometimes, lamb skins were oiled during the drying stage, to make them transparent, and used as windows for houses or lanterns.[17]

Stretching a sheep skin on a frame as it dries causes the fibres to separate into layers that can be separated into thinner sheets. On the other hand, the tanning process used to produce leather meshes the fibres into a single thick layer. The best vellum was said to be that made from aborted lambs or calves before the hairs had pierced the skin. A sheet of vellum (parchment) was folded once to form a quarto, or 3 times to give an octavo (20 x 25.5cm). An entire sheet of velum was 40 x 51cm, which is the maximum size that can be obtained from a sheepskin the size of a Soay type sheep![17]

Deeds and indentured documents were usually written on vellum. The word 'indentured' refers to documents cut in half with jagged edges. This enabled the holders of either half to prove if it was genuine because the cut edge of one half would only match that of the other half. An interesting example of an indentured bond on vellum is the one used as a cover for the Estate Accounts for Corva Manor (which included land in Zennor, Morvah and Sennen) from 1677 to 1691.[3] The Indentured Bond, dated the 10th of May 1665, was between Walter Moyle, Knight of Bake, of St. Germans and Samuel Palmer (yeoman) and his wife, of Cuttiviet in the Parish of Landrake, for an 80 year lease of land. However, there is no financial arrangement mentioned in the bond and although the document was used as a cover for the Corva Manor Accounts the deed is not mentioned in the accounts. Consequently, whether the document was simply recycled as a cover for the pages, or whether it had a legal significance to Corva Manor is a mystery that would provide an interesting item for future research.

Acknowledgements and References: I particularly wish to thank Mrs. Margaret Stuart of Walls, Shetland, and Peter McDonald of Creiff, Scotland for their help on spinning, spinning wheels and weaving.

1. Baines, P. 1977. Spinning Wheels, Spinner and Spinning. Batsford.
2. British Sheep, Eighth Edition. 1992 The National Sheep Assoc. (British).
3. Buller, Richard. 1677-91. Financial Accounts of Corva Manor (following his death) CRO.
4. Carew. 1602 Carew's Survey of Cornwall. pG3.
5. Cooke, I.M. 1996. Mermaid To Merrymaid. Journey To The Stones. Cornwall Litho, Redruth.
6. Davis, S.J.M. 1995 (reprint) The Archaeology of Animals. Batsford.
7. Edward Michell 1675 CRO M 1067/1-2 1 small fulling gown 10s.
8. English, W. 1969. The Textile Industry. Longmans.
9. Green, G. Personal communication. 1997.
10. Harlan, J.R. 1995. The Living Fields. Our Agricultural Heritage. Cambridge.
11. John Perry. A turn 2s 1675 CRO P1358/1-2.
12. Johnson, N. and P. Rose. 1990 Cornwall's Archaeological Heritage. Twelveheads Press, Truro.
13. Muir, R. 1990. The English Village. Thames and Hudson.
14. Quinnell, H. 1996. Personal communication, Exeter University.
15. Poole, P.A.S. 1981 The Tithings of Cornwall. p275-337. Journ. Royal Inst. Cornwall. Vol III, Part 4.
16. Poole, P.A.S. 1959 The Penhelig Manuscripts. p163-227. Journ. Royal Inst. Cornwall. Vol. 111. Part 3.
17. Ryder, M.L. 1983. Sheep and Man. Duckworth.
18. Taylor, Cannon. (Vicar of St. Just in Penwith) Unpublished notes on Cornish Manors.
19. Tonkin, T. 1811. Comments on Carew's 1602 Survey of Cornwall. p77-79.
20. Weatherhill, C. 1981 Bellerion Ancient Sites of Land's End. Alison Hodge, Penzance.
21. Whetter, J. 1991. Cornish Weather and Cornish People. Lyfro Trelyspen, St. Austell.
22. William Thomas. 23 fleeces July 1683 £1 CRO AP/T 1301.

Morvah Parish. Neolithic sheep and Chun Quoit *(Chapter VI)*.

Zennor Parish. Field patterns at Bosigran *(Chapter V)*.

Zennor Parish. Wicca Farm House *(Chapter V)*. **Built in the early 17th Century.**

Wicca ancient field patterns *(Chapter V)*.

Zennor Parish Bridge House (now Wayside Museum) may have been the home of Thomas Tregurtha *(Chapter V)*. **The eaves have been raised above the original height.**

Open hearth at Bridge House (now Wayside Museum).

Pendeen Manor (*Chapters II, III, V*). Home of John Borlase, gent. Left hand side of house is older. 1670 is the date on the chimney when improvements were being made.

Zennor Parish. Ruined 1-hearth cottage on Zennor Carn.

Towednack Parish Church *(Chapter VIII)*.

St. Just in Penwith Parish Church *(Chapter IX)*.

Sennen Parish. The Quaker Burial Ground *(Chapter X)* **is a walled rectangular enclosure 54ft. long by 46ft. wide on a solitary moorland location.**

The only visible grave is a massive slab of dressed granite 5ft. 7in. long, 2ft. wide and 1ft. thick resting on rough pieces of granite. The inscription carved into the 4 sides of the slab reads: "Here is buried that Virtuous woman Phillip the Wife of John Ellis who departed this life The XX Day of X month of 1677.

Boskenna Manor *(Chapter XI)* **as it is today. It was a fairly small house in 1680 but it was altered and enlarged considerably in the 19th Century.**

Gable of Boskenna Manor *(Chapter XI)*.

VII THE MERCHANTS OF PENZANCE

MARGARET E. PERRY

In May 1660 Charles II was proclaimed king. Penzance celebrated the restoration of the monarchy, spending £6.10s.6d on wine and a further £1 on beer for the musketeers[1]. The town, mainly loyal to the Royalist cause, had twice suffered at the hands of Parliamentary soldiers during the Civil War. In 1646 the town was ransacked after townspeople sheltered Royalist troops. Two years later a Penzance merchant, Anthony Gubbs, who supported the Parliamentarian cause and had suffered at the hands of local Royalists as a result, warned of a planned Royalist rebellion in the town. Initially little notice was taken of his complaints but eventually some of the ringleaders of the rebellion were arrested. Despite this on the night of the 16th May insurrection broke out. Royalist rebels seized Anthony Gubbs who described his treatment at their hands.[2]

"I was seased and my goodes confiscated for the supplie of ther rebellions & [feared] my life to be lost for which Grose, Madderne, Pike & others satt in Judgement one me because I would not supplie them with £300 for my life & had not God timely sent ayde I had lost my estate and life besides the Goodes they then forsed from me out of my shop and warehouses.

On the 22nd May, a Parliamentary force having been mustered, the rebels were attacked in Penzance and overcome. The Royalist leaders escaped to Mullion where the Parliamentary forces put down a further rebellion on The Lizard. They again plundered Penzance and in Penryn paraded their spoils and prisoners through the town.

The people of Penzance had lived through political change and unrest to reach the 1660s. Some still alive would have experienced the Spanish raid of 1595, many would have heard firsthand accounts. Roads were bad and most traffic was by sea, but this also brought danger. Raids along the Cornish coast by Moorish pirates from North Africa, referred to as 'Turks' were frequent and greatly feared, as men, boats and possessions were seized. The Calendars of State Papers for the 1660s and '70s highlight some of the ever present dangers.[3]

8th April 1667. Some French men-of-war have pestered the coast lately, and taken divers small merchantmen, some considerable laden. Several of the King's frigates lay meanwhile in Plymouth harbour, which causes some grumbling. *(1667 p.21)*
6th February 1673. Last Sunday night the Half-Moon of Dantzic, a ship of 350 tons, laden with salt and brandy, struck on the Eddystone and immediately sunk, but the men preserved themselves in their boat and got ashore near Looe *(1672-3 p.522)*
30th January 1674. Last Friday evening three small vessels were cast away going into Penzance, one belonging to that place, the others to St. Ives. They all came from Plymouth with deals and grocery ware. The men were all preserved and most of the goods *(1673-5 pp 126-7)*

Press gangs also presented a threat, an entry for the 1st February 1672 reads 'Our seamen are much afraid of being pressed, hearing that several about Plymouth are already taken up for the service.' In 1652, Eliasaph, one of the sons of Alexander Daniel who was then Lord of the Manor, merchant and a principal landowner in Penzance, had been pressed into the Commonwealth Navy. An apprentice in the art of navigation he was later to sail with his brother, Alexander, to the East and West Indies. Alexander never returned, dying on 31st October 1658 at Huglioe on the River Ganges, the site of the Merchant Venturers Factory, where he had gone to trade.[4] Eliasaph was with him when he died, returning to Penzance in 1661 where, in 1665, he married Jane, daughter of John Penrose of Madron. Their father recorded the dates of their journeys and major family events.[5]

Sickness took its toll, the town was visited by plague in 1647 and the Parish Register records 150 burials in that year, compared with 30 in 1646.[6] Among the victims were three children of Penzance merchant, Robert Harry and his wife, Christian. Following her death at an early age Robert married Elizabeth Usticke of St. Just. There were a number of children of this marriage but Elizabeth died in 1677, to be followed in 1681 by Robert who had married for the third time in the interim period. In his will he names his wife as Dorothy, leaving her only a token legacy as he had provided for her in the marriage settlement.[7] At the time of his death, aged 76 years, all of the children of the second marriage were under age. Robert Harry was a prosperous merchant, his estate, as listed in his inventory, valued at £485.[8] The inventory records that his house had eleven rooms and the 1664 Hearth Tax Returns show seven chargeable hearths.[9] Edmund, the eldest child of Robert and Elizabeth, inherited property at Treneere from his uncle, John Usticke.

The occasion of the coronation of Charles II in October 1660 provided an opportunity to look forward to a more secure future. Inhabitants celebrated in style. Corporation accounts for that year record expenditure of £20.9s on celebrating the event, including '£1 for a Boate that was burnt at the coronation.[10] There are two other related items of expenditure, 9s. was paid to the High Constable towards the `repayration of Looe and Seaton bridges,' and `Paid for the Kings Rent £3.6s.8d.' A curious entry among the above, but not specifically referring in so many words to the coronation, was payment to the Parliamentary supporter Anthony Gubbs for powder. It must be supposed that he did not join in the celebrations, or perhaps he did? Alexander Daniel attempted to avoid involvement in political issues with little success. For a time he served, with his eldest son Richard, in the Royalist forces before Plymouth and in 1644 he was compelled, under threat of imprisonment, to pay £30 to the Royal coffers. He took no part in the Royalist uprising of 1648 so was naturally aggrieved when attacked by Parliamentarian soldiers who took his money and horse, which he was later forced to buy back for £3.[11] He wrote that he had been going to Penzance at the time of the attack to congratulate the Parliamentary captains on their success!

Alexander Daniel died in 1668 having seen his son Richard, who took little interest in his Cornish properties, sell the Lordship and the remaining properties of Alverton to William Keigwin in 1664 for £250. Anthony Gubbs died in 1662, he had been mayor in 1645 and 1656 and one of his sons, Joseph, in 1651, 1652 and 1659.[12] The family continued to prosper as merchants in Penzance. The eldest son, also Anthony, issued a farthing token in 1667 and was Assistant Stannator in 1664.[13]

AN ARTIST'S IMPRESSION OF THE WEST FRONT OF PENZANCE MARKET HOUSE IN THE 17th CENTURY.

In 1660 Penzance had been a borough for nearly fifty years, receiving its Charter of Incorporation from King James I in 1614, nineteen years after Marazion. These towns, together with Mousehole, were the main ports on the western side of Mount's Bay prior to the Spanish raid of 1595. Mousehole never recovered its former status but Penzance continued to grow and prosper. Rivalry continued between Penzance and Marazion but the advantages of Penzance harbour over that of the Mount probably acted in favour of Penzance, as did the granting, in 1663, of the Coinage Charter. Problems of transporting heavy blocks of tin over poor roads to Helston, and the rapid development of mining in the St. Just area were principal factors in the declaration of Penzance as a stannary town. Among rights and privileges granted by the Charter of Incorporation were weekly markets, fairs, with the confirmation of harbour rights, previously granted by Henry VIII in 1512. Rents of markets, fairs and the quay formed the main source of revenue for the newly formed Corporation. The mayors of the borough had always included a large number of merchants, men of influence, and usually of substance and property. During the twenty-five year reign of Charles II at least thirteen mayors are known to have been merchants, possibly there were more. They would, having completed their time as mayor, remain as Justices of the Peace for a further year and continue to serve as aldermen.[14]

It is possible to form a picture of Penzance in the year 1660. The bounds of the borough had been defined as a half-mile radius from the middle of the town, measured from the point in the Green Market where the Cross stood. Even within this comparatively small area a large proportion of the land was agricultural or waste. The population of Penzance at this time is not recorded, and is difficult to calculate using the few statistics available. In the 1642 Protestation Return 243 males over 18 are listed for Penzance. Hearth Tax records for 1664 list 218 chargeable hearths in 103 households, however many were exempt from this tax and variations in the size of the household need to be taken into account. Parish records are incomplete for this period but the population of Penzance would certainly have been rather less than one thousand persons. Whetter estimates the population at a figure as low as 594 (in 1662)[15] and refers to the main towns of the county as being little more than overgrown villages. Statistics can come from unexpected sources, the chart reproduced below shows the seating plan for St. Mary's Chapel for the year 1674.[16] Some 220 people are listed but these do not include children and it seems likely that all on the chart are persons of some standing, including the merchants who are among those given the courtesy title of 'Mr.' There would have been additional seating for the poor of the community and some attended the mother church of Madron.

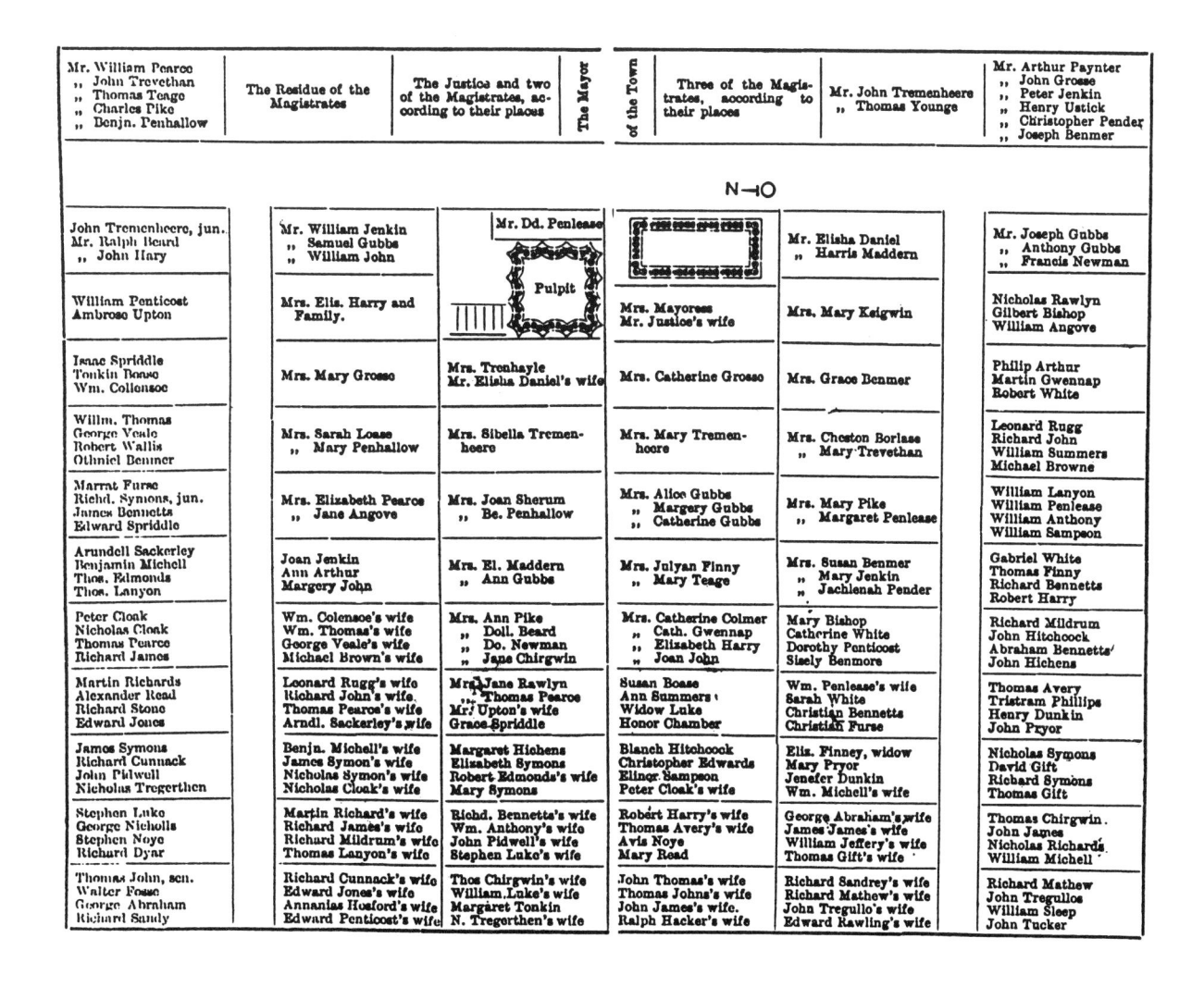

Mr. William Pearce " John Trevethan " Thomas Teage " Charles Pike " Benjn. Penhallow	The Residue of the Magistrates	The Justice and two of the Magistrates, according to their places	The Mayor of the Town	Three of the Magistrates, according to their places	Mr. John Tremenheere " Thomas Younge	Mr. Arthur Paynter " John Grosse " Peter Jenkin " Henry Ustick " Christopher Pender " Joseph Benmer
			N→O			
John Tremenheere, jun. Mr. Ralph Beard " John Hary	Mr. William Jenkin " Samuel Gubbs " William John	Mr. Dd. Penlease Pulpit		Mr. Elisha Daniel " Harris Maddern		Mr. Joseph Gubbs " Anthony Gubbs " Francis Newman
William Penticost Ambrose Upton	Mrs. Eliz. Harry and Family.			Mrs. Mayoress Mr. Justice's wife	Mrs. Mary Keigwin	Nicholas Rawlyn Gilbert Bishop William Angove
Isaac Spriddle Tonkin Boase Wm. Collensoe	Mrs. Mary Grosse	Mrs. Trenhayle Mr. Elisha Daniel's wife		Mrs. Catherine Grosse	Mrs. Grace Benmer	Philip Arthur Martin Gwennap Robert White
Willm. Thomas George Veale Robert Wallis Othniel Benmer	Mrs. Sarah Loase " Mary Penhallow	Mrs. Sibella Tremenheere		Mrs. Mary Tremenheere	Mrs. Cheston Borlase " Mary Trevethan	Leonard Rugg Richard John William Summers Michael Browne
Marrat Furse Richd. Symons, jun. James Bennetts Edward Spriddle	Mrs. Elizabeth Pearce " Jane Angove	Mrs. Joan Sherum " Be. Penhallow		Mrs. Alice Gubbs " Margery Gubbs " Catherine Gubbs	Mrs. Mary Pike " Margaret Penlease	William Lanyon William Penlease William Anthony William Sampson
Arundell Sackerley Benjamin Michell Thos. Edmonds Thos. Lanyon	Joan Jenkin Ann Arthur Margery John	Mrs. El. Maddern " Ann Gubbs		Mrs. Julyan Finny " Mary Teage	Mrs. Susan Benmer " Mary Jenkin " Jachlenah Pender	Gabriel White Thomas Finny Richard Bennetts Robert Harry
Peter Cloak Nicholas Cloak Thomas Pearce Richard James	Wm. Colensoe's wife Wm. Thomas's wife George Veale's wife Michael Brown's wife	Mrs. Ann Pike " Doll. Beard " Do. Newman " Jane Chirgwin		Mrs. Catherine Colmer " Cath. Gwennap " Elizabeth Harry " Joan John	Mary Bishop Catherine White Dorothy Penticost Sisely Benmore	Richard Mildrum John Hitchcock Abraham Bennetts John Hichens
Martin Richards Alexander Read Richard Stone Edward Jones	Leonard Rugg's wife Richard John's wife Thomas Pearce's wife Arndl. Sackerley's wife	Mr. Jane Rawlyn " Thomas Pearce Mr. Upton's wife Grace Spriddle		Susan Boase Ann Summers Widow Luke Honor Chamber	Wm. Penlease's wife Sarah White Christian Bennetts Christian Furse	Thomas Avery Tristram Phillips Henry Dunkin John Pryor
James Symons Richard Cunnack John Pidwell Nicholas Tregerthen	Benjn. Michell's wife James Symon's wife Nicholas Symon's wife Nicholas Cloak's wife	Margaret Hichens Elizabeth Symons Robert Edmonds's wife Mary Symons		Blanch Hitchcock Christopher Edwards Elinor Sampson Peter Cloak's wife	Eliz. Finney, widow Mary Pryor Jenefer Dunkin Wm. Michell's wife	Nicholas Symons David Gift Richard Symons Thomas Gift
Stephen Luke George Nicholls Stephen Noye Richard Dyar	Martin Richard's wife Richard James's wife Richard Mildrum's wife Thomas Lanyon's wife	Richd. Bennetts's wife Wm. Anthony's wife John Pidwell's wife Stephen Luke's wife		Robert Harry's wife Thomas Avery's wife Avis Noye Mary Read	George Abraham's wife James James's wife William Jeffery's wife Thomas Gift's wife	Thomas Chirgwin John James Nicholas Richards William Michell
Thomas John, sen. Walter Fosse George Abraham Richard Sandy	Richard Cunnack's wife Edward Jones's wife Annanias Hosford's wife Edward Penticost's wife	Thos Chirgwin's wife William Luke's wife Margaret Tonkin N. Tregerthen's wife		John Thomas's wife Thomas Johns's wife John James's wife Ralph Hacker's wife	Richard Sandrey's wife Richard Mathew's wife John Tregullo's wife Edward Rawling's wife	Richard Mathew John Tregullos William Sleep John Tucker

In early days the town developed from a cluster of houses built around the quay below St. Mary's Chapel and around the chapel itself. A good indication of this is gained from a map of Mount's Bay of 1515.[17] The chapel steeple was whitewashed and served as a landmark for seamen. Following the granting of the Charter in 1614 the Corporation purchased from Richard Daniel, a Truro merchant and Lord of the Manor of Alverton, a three-cornered plot of land together with the right of income from all fairs, markets and the stone quay and harbour. On one side was built the Market House, Guildhall and Borough prison, the others formed what is now Market Place but was then an extension of Chapel Street. It was here that merchants looked to build new homes and businesses. One was John Tremenheere who lived in a house referred to as 'The Mansion of the Tremenheeres.' This was probably built by his father, Henry, who moved to Penzance from Helston as a young man to follow a commercial career in the developing port.[18] He was mayor of Penzance in 1643, the year of his death. The Tremenheeres became one of the leading merchant families of Penzance.

ST. MARY'S CHAPEL

Houses of little consequence straggled down Market Jew Street for a short distance and more substantial properties were found in Chapel Street (then Lady Street). The main concentration of building was around the quay where fish cellars were erected. The water front, which at that time consisted of the towans (sandhills) was far more extensive than today. The land was used for grazing cattle, drying nets and related activities. Following the granting of the Coinage Charter in 1663 the Corporation built a Coinage Hall on ground adjoining the east end of the Market House and at about the same time an alms-house was built on the north side of Market Jew Street. The chapel was rebuilt in 1672 and consecrated in 1680 'as a Chapel of Ease to the Vicarial Church of Madern,' having previously been licensed from time to time by the Bishops of Exeter. The merchant John Tremenheere gave land that made consecration possible, the rent from it being used to support a curate.[19] When he died in 1686 John had been building his 'new brick house' on land adjoining the chapel, brick built houses being considered superior to granite.[20] Other gifts to the chapel included a granite font, given by Grace Benmer in 1668. She was the wife of the merchant Thomas Benmer and the font was possibly given to mark the deaths of two of their children, Thomas in 1658 and John in 1662. The couple had a daughter, Rebecca, who was born in 1663, but there are no records of other sons. Thomas Benmer was Mayor of Penzance in the years 1664, 1671 and 1679. On the 1674 seating plan Grace Benmer has her own pew, her husband is not shown by name probably because he was a magistrate at the time. It can be seen from the chart that husbands and wives were segregated in church. Thomas Benmer features in the Corporation Accounts as a supplier of goods and in the port books he is shown importing salt from France.[21] He died in 1691 and his inventory, total £50.17s.6d.,[22] shows he enjoyed a high standard of living.

The increasing importance of Penzance brought a number of merchants into the town. Henry Tremenheere of Helston has already been mentioned. His son John, following the death of his first wife, married Sibella, widow of Thomas Worth of Penryn. The Worths were a wealthy merchant family, originally from Barnstaple, and Sibella inherited considerable estate from her first husband. Some complex family relationships ensued as the two sons of John Tremenheere by his first marriage, Henry and John, married their step-mother's daughter and grand-daughter (also Sibella) respectively.[23] Another to move to Penzance was John Cleverdon, a mercer who issued a farthing token bearing his name and the Mercers' Arms. He and Nicholas Shearme, who was Mayor of Penzance on five occasions, possibly came from Kilkhampton, Stratton or Morwenstow where their surnames were relatively common. The inventory of John Cleverdon on his death in 1667 totalled £575, with debts of £468.13s.4d.[24] He owed £43 to Anthony Gubbs, Jnr. and £100 to Peter Hallamore, who was married to Tamsin Gubbs, daughter of the elder Anthony. The Hallamores were a prosperous merchant family in Penryn in the early 17th century. Madron parish register for this period gives little indication of trade, the term 'merchant' occurs just twenty times, but from there and other sources it has been possible to compile a list of merchants trading in Penzance during the reign of Charles II. One of these, Walter Fynny, was born before 1624, as he was able to sign the 1642 Protestation Return, and was mayor in 1658. When he died in 1671 the inventory of his possessions totalled £479, a considerable sum.[25] In the 1664 Hearth Tax he is listed as having six hearths and the inventory lists his house as having a parlour, kitchen, hall and buttery, with four chambers over these rooms. Several leases totalled £90 and his 'boats and appurtences' were valued at £100. There were `new' and `old' cellars with salt, barrels, etc., and he owned `a halfen deale of a small Barke called the Anthony' valued at £20. The port books of 1667/68 show the *Anthony* of 12 tons, captained by Othniel Benmer, trading to France with cargoes of pilchards and returning with salt.[26] Walter Fynny was a Penzance merchant able to finance fishing boats and the curing of fish, while importing salt, casks and other necessities and transporting fish to France. He owned a quay and pier at Penzance which he purchased from Alexander Daniel.

The wills and inventories of Penzance merchants show that they maintained cellars and warehouses and, although they used public quays, they sometimes owned private ones. The wealthier merchants, such as Bryan Rogers of Falmouth, bought pilchards from Henry Tremenheere, Joseph Gubbs and other merchants in the Penzance area. Using larger vessels they were able to export to Mediterranean countries and beyond. John Tremenheere and Peter Jenkyn were among Penzance merchants exporting increasing quantities of tin but they, and other merchants also traded in a wide range of goods. In 1687 the port books record the conveyance to London of goatskins, pewter and `trayn oil,' a by-product of pilchard curing. The pewter was possibly produced by Joseph Benmer, a pewterer recorded as working in Penzance during the second half of the 17th century.[27] Imports from France recorded in 1667 include iron and brass domestic ware, window glass, wine and vinegar. Anthony Gubbs, Jnr. imported 3,500 pounds of tobacco from Virginia in August of that year. Mixed cargoes of foodstuffs and other consumer goods were always in transit along the coast, sometimes recorded as '4 tons grocery ware' but at other times itemised. In 1686/7 a shipment from Plymouth included tobacco, dried fruit, sugar, spirits, English brandy, hops, lymes, paper, dried fish, soap, deal boards and brown candy. There were regular deliveries of goods from Penzance to the Isles of Scilly.[28] Markets and fairs had been the usual places for exchange of goods but by the 1660s trading was increasingly taking place in shops. However, generally markets were regarded as superior to shops or craft workshops.

MERCHANTMAN ARRIVING IN PENZANCE

The 17th century merchant was an educated man, sent to school and then apprenticed to a merchant, possibly in London. Apprentice merchants were frequently sent abroad to further their commercial experience and learn foreign languages, principally French, Spanish and Dutch. Latin was taught as a subject at school. The Penzance merchants were men of influence and power, they often traded internally as well as importing and exporting goods. They employed agents in the ports to which they traded and acted as agents for merchants of other ports. Merchants owned shares in mines and boats, both merchant and fishing. They financed tinners and fishermen, in the latter case advancing money against seasonal catches. Granting credit or lending money could be a good investment. They also acquired property, both for use in their business and as investment. Trade was not always legal, customs duty was high and tin, wines, spirits and cloth were smuggled. Customs officials could sometimes be bribed and were often inefficient. Thomas Young, the Collector of the Customs at Penzance in the 1680s, was an active merchant and allowed the smuggling of goods. Merchants transported tin by small boats at night to vessels waiting in Mount's Bay. The trade was said to be 'chiefly managed and carried on by the Two Tremenears who are brothers and live at Penzance.'[29] The Tremenheeres were an eminent local family, but merchants in the 17th century did not seem to consider illegal trade necessarily dishonest. Trade increased in Penzance during the reign of Charles II. The growth of mining in the locality brought business and helped to further the town's growing importance as a trading port. Fishing prospered. The merchants were prominent citizens, holding office in the town and with wealth and possessions often equalling those of local landed gentry. This would perhaps change as the town moved into the 18th century but 1660-1685 was, for the most part, a good time to be a Penzance merchant.

Some Penzance Merchants in the late 1600's

Ralph Beard (issued farthing token 1667)	Martyn Gwennap
Thomas Benmer (Mayor 1664,71 & 79)	Robert Harry (Mayor 1672,78)
John Blunt (issued farthing token 1665)	Peter Jenken (Mayor 1685,91)
John Cleverdon (issued farthing token)	Martin Maddern (Mayor 1662,70)
Alexander Daniel	Nicholas Shearme (Mayor 1636,43,46,60,68)
Walter Fynny (Mayor 1658)	John Tremenheere (Mayor 1655) John
Anthony Gubbs (Mayor 1645,56)	Tremenheere, Jnr. (Mayor 1686,90,97)
Anthony Gubbs, Jnr. (issued farthing token 1667)	Henry Tremenheere (Mayor 1674,82)
Joseph Gubbs (Mayor 1651,52,59)	John Treveathen (Mayor 1681, issued farthing token)
Sampson Gubbs	Thomas Tyag

REFERENCES
1. Penzance Corporation Accounts. CRO/DC/PEN/305
2. Cornish Weather & Cornish People in the 17th Century - James Whetter p.104
3. Old Cornwall Vol VI No.12 Spring 1967 pp 546 - 556
4. The Tremenheeres - Seymour Greig Tremenheere p.42. Morrab Library
5. Briefe Chronological Observations. Transcribed by George Millett 1874. Morrab Library
6. First Book of Madron Parish Registers. Morrab Library
7. CRO/AP/H/2014/1
8. CRO/AP/H/2014/2
9. Cornwall Hearth & Poll Taxes 1660 - 1664. Bristol 1981.
10. CRO/DC/PEN/305
11. Autobiography of Alexander Daniel of Alverton (1599-1668) P.A.S. Pool. RIC Journal Vol.VII pp 262-275
12. History of the Town & Borough of Penzance. P.A.S. Pool 1974 pp 278-283
13. Cornish Tokens. J.A.Williams (pub. D. Bradford Barton) pp 21-22
14. History of Penzance - Pool II The Old Borough 1614-1714
15. Cornwall in the 17th Century -James Whetter (Lodenek Press 1974) p.8
16. Penzance: Past and Present. George Bown Millett 1876. Morrab Library
17. British Museum MSS Cotton Augustus 1i 34. Reproduced as plate 1 in History of Penzance (Pool)
18. The Tremenheere. Morrab Library
19. History of Penzance (Pool) p.52
20. The Tremenheeres p.42. Morrab Library
21. CRO/AD/479/2 Transcripts of Port Books
22. CRO/B/2256/1,2
23. Penryn in the 17th Century - June Palmer 1986
24. CRO/C/1429/1,2
25. CRO/F/2941/2
26. CRO/AD/479/2
27. Cornwall in the 17th Century - Whetter -p.21
28. CRO\AD/79\229. Cornwall in the 17th Century.

VIII FAMILIES AND NEIGHBOURS IN TOWEDNACK
CONNECTIONS AND CONFLICTS

ELSA CLEE

Few Cornish families, it has been said, can vie with Rosewall in point of antiquity. A homestead called Rosewall on the eastern side of Rosewall Hill, Towednack (Plate 6a), was occupied by the family for generations. The Subsidy Roll of 1327 included the names of John de Ryswal and Noal de Ryswal of Towednack in connection with 2 shillings each paid towards the royal aid. [1]

Of a total of approximately 15 Inventories available for Towednack for the period 1660-1691, [2] that of Andrew Roswall[3] has the highest value with £354.8.6, the only others to approach it being: Robert Curnow[4] £196.14. 8, Francis Quick [5] £150. 3. 4.

Land figured largely in Andrew Roswall's Inventory - namely to the value of £265.0.0, and included a tenement in Lelant, called Venven; a moiety of Roswall in Towednack and an Estate in the Borisas.[6] In his will, Andrew provided for his six daughters, Chesten, Mary, Margrey, Willmott, Ann and Elizabeth - 'Twenty Pounds apece to each of them six months after the days of theire respective maradges'. Mary, his 'deere and loveing Wife' was also well provided for, as were James, his brother, James's two children and Andrew's godchildren. To the poor of the parish of 'Towidnacke' he left 20 shillings. The impression of close family ties is reinforced by the bequest of twenty pounds to his sister, Mary, for her use and that of her son, to be paid twelve months after his death. Discord is, however, revealed by Andrew Roswall's proviso that Mary's husband, Hugh Rosemenewes, '...shall have nothing to do with the same.' The twenty pounds was to be laid out to interest or any other ways 'ffor the good of my said sister and her son as ffrancis Arundell of Trengwanton Gent... (described as 'my very good freind') shall think fitt...'

The impression given of a strong character, hinted at in Andrew's dealings with his brother-in-law, is strengthened by his refusal to pay tithes, which resulted in a law suit in 1679. Religious fervour had subsided somewhat after 1660, but ill-feeling was prevalent among the parishioners of Lelant, St. Ives and Towednack. These parishes were represented by one vicar, who was frequently absent, and whose duties can only be described as 'light'. The custom of demanding full tithes was, nevertheless, still firmly in place. Depositions of witnesses concerning Andrew Roswall were taken in the first instance at the 'House of Thomas Tonkyn Vintner scituate within the village of Newlyn in the parish of Paull...' before Thomas Hicks Esq., ffrancis Paynter gent., Ezechiell Arundell and ffrancis Arundell Esqrs., and between John Hawkyns, clerk, and Andrewe Roswall, defendant. James Quicke of Zennor, yeoman, aged 48, stated that the defendant "doth depasture his cattell on the tenemt called Rosewall and on that pte of the tenemt called Boreesa"[6]. The defendant was also stated to "likewise keepe and depasture on the said premisses three or ffower labouring horses...and doth usually imploy them in carryinge of tyn stuffe to the stampinge Mill and also to the bloweing howse". Thomas Hodge of Towednack, yeoman, aged 50, confirmed that Andrew Roswall also held Bregia Vean or Borisa Vean, the land being described by John Hickes of St. Ives as "very course and barren".

FOUR LABOURING HORSES

James Trewhela of Towednack, yeoman, aged 65, alleged that Andrew Roswall wanted him to join him in resisting the tithes at Law, but Trewhela refused. According to Thomas Quick, aged 34, of Towednack, Roswall had been concerned in three several law suits. William Andrew of Saint Earth, yeoman, was particularly disparaging in his citing of an instance when the Defendant "hath lately prosecuted severall vexatious Law suites against John Gyles". It was asserted that Gyles was coerced into passing over some other land to Roswall.

Such proceedings could hardly have fostered good neighbourly feelings within the community. In his deposition, Alexander Odger, yeoman, aged 27, for example, stated that he was with Mary Hodge and Thomas Hodge, yeoman, her husband, at the house of ffrancis Trewhella in Towidnacke. Thomas spoke to his wife saying "I have wronged Andrew Roswall in his concerns with Mr. Hawkinge" (presumably John Hawkyns, Vicar, Complainant) "and thou hast wronged him allsoe". To this Mary Hodge replied "Hold your Tongue, I will sweare any thinge that comes upon my mynd".[1] This Mary Hodge was the same formidable lady who, according to Alse Richards, spinster, aged 53, of Towednack, had come into her house and sat "...by the ffire there Smoakinge a pipe of tobaccoe...".

In the Towednack Wills and Inventories, further tension is revealed in the will of Anne Wadge in 1662.[7] Money was left to members of her family, Nottell cousins, the Phillipes and Renoden families and to the poor of the parish. However, another item in the will reads 'Sixt poundes to my cossen Margrett Tregerthen, widow, and her children but her eldest son his (sic) to have nothing of that Sixt poundes'.

WOMAN ENJOYING A PIPE OF TOBACCO

The fact that land and possessions were frequently only partly owned was a potential source of conflict. James Roswall in his 1680 Inventory [8] included 'the half of an old brass pan' valued at 4 shillings, while among William Russell's goods in 1661 [9] 'the one halfe of a Nag(e) £1.10.0.' is mentioned. Debts were often outstanding at the time of death, and could be considerable. Those listed as owing to Francis Quick, for example, amounted to £38.0.0. out of his total goods and chattels of £150.3.4. If left unsettled, quarrels were bound to result.

In years to come, rivalry arose between the Stevens, the Quicks and the Michells over an incident in c.1470. The Stevens (or Stephens) were thought to have been descended from an Irish farmer who was shipwrecked at Wicka Pool, Zennor. The Michells and the Quicks maintained that they owned the cattle being carried at the time of shipwreck - Stevens merely being the drover. One of the Stevens family's most famous sons (or rather, daughters), Zenobia Stevens - alias Baragwanath, (born 1661; died 1763 at the age of 102) lived at Trevisa Wartha. Zenobia's story may not be new to many, but in the hope that a twice-told tale will not be tedious[10] the brief facts are that at the age of nearly 99, her lease of 99 years held under the Duke of Bolton, was about to expire. Her mind, however, was put at rest on going to see her lawyer. Zenobia partook of one glass of wine, but refused a second. It was getting dark - she had to ride home on a young colt - and was afraid she might become light-headed. [1 and 15]

REFUSING MORE WINE...

A family connection may exist between Zenobia Stevens and two names which appear as appraisers of Towednack inventories. Matthew Stevens appraised Francis Quick's inventory in 1689 and those of James and Andrew Roswall in 1680. The inventory of John Paul,[11] who was the father-in-law of Francis Quick, was appraised by William Steephin in 1662.

There is no doubt that folks in this period lived in interesting times. Registers available for Towednack Parish only began in 1676 [12]. There is consequently no evidence as to the effect the plague and famine of 1646-7 had on Towednack when in St. Ives one-third (535) of the population died. There is evidence that some families at least were reasonably well situated economically. Mary Hodge, (if her deposition can be relied upon!) maintained that she usually made 5½ pounds of butter from the milk of one cow in a week. Dr. Whetter calculated that three gallons of milk made one pound of butter so Mary Hodges' cow was producing a good yield of two gallons of milk a day.[13]

QUIETENING A YOUNG COLT.

In 1660, The Borough Accounts for St. Ives contain many items connected with the Restoration - disbursements for mainly correspondence and conviviality - for example, 'Imprimis pd. the king's Coronation day to Cockin to beate the drum 2s. 6d.' Various allusions are made to liquid refreshment 'ffor beere the coronation day' ranging from 5s.0d. to 13s.0d. However, one item 'pd. to Symon ffor castinge three dead dogs out of the River 3d.' would appear to bear little relationship to the festivities in hand.

Families and neighbours in the region of Towednack were divided in their political affiliations during the Civil War, and such divisions would not disappear overnight. After riots which took place in St. Ives, Sir Richard Grenville, the Royalist Commander, regarded Truro, Helston and St. Ives as "the three most rotten Towns in the West", believing they had supported the Parliamentarian cause. In 1645, a rising of the inhabitants of St. Ives, Zennor and Towednack on Longstone Downs, under their leader, Captain Robert Arundell, was ruthlessly suppressed. One man was hanged at Truro; another at Helston, and a third at St. Ives.[14]

The St. Ives Borough Accounts reveal more than disbursements for beer and paying the piper and the fiddlers. In 1645, six pence had been paid to the one who did 'whipp the mayde that would drown herself'. Whereas in 1665/6 twice that, one shilling, was paid for whipping Mary Renoden.

A WHIPPING.

A family connection exists, perhaps, with Ann Wadge, whose will we have examined. Mary's misdemeanour was not referred to - a disadvantage if curiosity is not allayed, or, alternatively, an advantage if the discomfiture of future generations is to be avoided.

Families with which the Renodens inter-married, as given in the Towednack Parish Registers, include Baragwanath, Berriman, Brown, Curnow, Hosking, Jeffery, Michell, Osborn, Quick, Thomas, Trewhella and Woolcock.

Who among us has not yearned for the simple pleasures of yesteryear and the closeness of family and community ties? A perusal of primary sources might provide the answer - a speedy antidote to the onset of nostalgia!

A BOSIGRAN COTTAGE, NOW DEMOLISHED, WITH ONE HEARTH. ILLUSTRATED WITH ROPED STRAW THATCH.

REFERENCES
(1) A History of the Parishes of St. Ives, Lelant, Towednack and Zennor.   John Hobson Matthews.
    Publ. London. Elliot Stock 1892
(2) Wills and Inventories 1660-1693 Towednack, CRO ACP/WR 185
(3) CRO R1163/2 Andrew Roswall
(4) CRO AP/C 1985/2 Robert Curnow
(5) CRO Q30/2 Francis Quick
(6) Borisas, Boreesa - BREJA , Breyssa 1580 Boreesa, Borissa 1680.   The Place-Names of
    West Penwith 2nd Ed. 1985 - P.A.S. Pool
(7) CRO W860/1 Anne Wadge
(8) CRO R1164/1-4. James Roswall
(9) CRO R8183   William Russell
(10) Shakespeare - King John. Act III Scene IV "...Life is as tedious as a twice-told tale..." (Lewis)
(11) CRO P1042/2 John Paul
(12) Baptisms, Burials & Marriages. Towednack Parish Registers 1676-1812. Morrab Library,   Morrab
    Gardens, Penzance. Transcribed by W.T. Hoblyn.
(13) An Economic History of Kernow in the 17th Century.   PRO.E.134 31 Chas.2 Mich 6
    James Whetter, B.A., Ph.D Publ. Lodenek Press 1974
(14) Cornwall in the Great Civil War and Interregnum 1642-1660 Mary Coate .A., F.S.A., FR.Hist.S
    Publ. D. Bradford Barton Ltd. Truro 1963
(15) Autobiography of a Cornish Rector. Rev. James Hamley Tregenna. Publ. in 2 vols. London
    Tinsley Bros. 18, Catherine St. Strand. 1872 Cornish Studies Library, Redruth

IX RICHARD ANGWIN OF ST. JUST IN PENWITH c. 1600 to 1675.

CARLENE HARRY

Richard Angwin was born about 1600 into a family that had been in West Penwith, if not in the parish of St. Just, for over one hundred years, although its origins there may well go back considerably further.

A Harry Angwin is mentioned in the Penheleg Manuscript[2] as giving evidence, at a Court held on 22 Feb 1564/5, about a wreck he had seen in 1530/1 at 'Senar Clyffe by Innyall Chappell'.[2] As he also said he often saw wreckage in 'Whitsonbay and other places about Land's End' he must have been a resident of the area and could well have lived in St. Just Parish. Other Angwins are mentioned in various documents throughout the 1500s.[3] These place the family mainly in St. Just but there was also a connection with the parish of Sancreed. Unfortunately there is not enough information to reconstruct the family so although it is almost certain that Richard and the Henry, born c.1489, were of the same family their actual relationship cannot be determined.

The early Angwins were prosperous, apparently owning rather than leasing land. One, a Martin, sometime in the early/mid 1500s, married Cecily, daughter of William Lanyon, and was the only non armorial bearing person to marry into that family at the time.[4] During the 1500s the Angwins, or at least some of them, lived at Bojewyan in St. Just like Richard some years later.

No description of Bojewyan in the 1600s exists but from documents a little is known about the settlement there. The house occupied by Martin, Richard's father, and later by Richard himself was large, having six hearths in 1664. Unfortunately the Hearth Tax does not indicate which other properties at Bojewyan were taxed although some must have been, including almost certainly, the 3 hearth house of Malachais Angwin. There may have been other untaxed cottages there too. A document dated 1641 refers to an indenture of 1610 that 'demised granted and confirmed unto Richard Angwin Martin Angwin the younger and Honor Angwin' part of Bojewyan which included some messuages (dwelling houses with outbuildings), old walls, gardens etc.[5] Other land Richard bought in 1670 included orchards and yards. The surrounding land was made up of crofts, fields, pasture, meadows, feedings, fursecrofts, heath, commons and moors with at least one of the fields divided into stitches.

Although no record of Richard's baptism survives, by 1671 when his will[7] was written, he describes himself as not only sick in body but also as "beinge aged". His father's will[8] indicates that he was the son of a Martin and Julyan, both of whom died in 1639, and that he had a brother Martin, and five sisters, Agnes, Jane, Honor, Catherine and Cecily. From the use of the names Martin and Cecily it seems likely that Richard was directly descended from Martin and Cecily, née Lanyon. He married Grace, baptised 1602, daughter of Thomas Fleming of Landithy, at Madron in 1646. There is no indication that there were any children of this marriage.

The Fleming family was originally from 'Monster' in Ireland. Grace's father Thomas, was the son of Nicholas and Elizabeth, daughter of Jenkin Keigwin of Paul. Her mother, Elizabeth, was the daughter of Thomas and Alice Cock of Bodmin.[9] There is a memorial on the wall of the Lady Chapel in Madron Church to Grace's father who died in 1631, and to her maternal grandparents, Thomas and Alice Cock, who died in 1601 and 1610 respectively. The slate slab depicts the standing figures of Grace's maternal grandparents and parents with kneeling figures of the latter's ten children, Nicholas, Thomas, John, Frances, Grace, Ann, Elizabeth, Mary and Phillipa. All are identified by their initials. The arms of both Thomas Cock and Thomas Fleming are also represented. Grace's mother Elizabeth died in 1650.

Richard would have brought his bride Grace to live at his house in Bojewyan. Although the family had lived there for sometime, from 1610 if not before, it had been leased from Henry Angwin and after his death from his son John until bought by Richard in 1642. In 1639 it was quite a substantial dwelling having a hall, parlour, kitchen, and buttery downstairs with chambers over each, that over the buttery being described as 'new'. There was also a store chamber over the entry.[10] By 1675 the house had been further enlarged by the addition of another buttery with a chamber over it. Here they would have lived comfortably with household servants to look after their needs.[12]

The hearth tax of 1664 indicates that Richard's house, having six hearths, was one of the largest in the parish. This meant that as well as hearths downstairs in the hall, parlour and kitchen, three rooms upstairs were heated, but which, and were they all used as bedrooms? Richard's inventory unfortunately, does not give details of items in the rooms but Martin's does and it lists a desk in the new chamber over the buttery. Was this room used as a study/office with a hearth to provide heat?

A GENTLEMAN AT HIS WRITING

At this period it is difficult to know about the standard of literacy. From their wills alone, which only bear their signs not their signatures, it is not possible to know whether Martin or Richard were literate. Martin's inventory indicates he had a desk which suggests an ability to write and it is known from other sources that Richard was, in fact, literate and when his signature appears on a document it is in a firm and clear hand. It is interesting to speculate whether Richard did his writing in the "new" room over the buttery where, in 1639 there was a desk, on a typical cold, damp, misty St. Just day, with the wind whistling around the house, being warmed by a roaring fire burning brightly in the hearth.

By the 1660s to 1670s Richard was one of the very few remaining speakers and writers of the Cornish language. Nicholas Boson, in his 'Nebbaz Gerriau Dro Tho Carnock',[13] refers to him as 'Sieur Angwin the greatest and eldest of the late professors of the Cornish Tongue'. He goes on to say however, that even Richard made mistakes, interpreting Gevern Anko as 'goats all'. Richard had forgotten that Gevern was the word for a Hundred. In fact Keverang is a Hundred, plural Keverango. He had confused it with the word for goat - gavar, a word with which he was familiar, a goat's head being his sealing devise.[14]

John Ray, the eminent naturalist visited West Penwith in 1662 and referred to him as "the only man" he heard of who could write and speak Cornish. In 1667 when John Ray was again in the area he actually visited Richard.[15] Being an Englishman he misinterpreted Richard's name which he recorded as Dickan Gwyn. The name Angwin is Cornish, an + gwyn meaning 'the white'. Why was this name taken or given? It might relate to some natural feature associated with their place of abode. Alternatively it might relate to a personal attribute such as fair hair or skin. Certainly some descendants of Richard's cousin Bennet have white skins that do not tan, but whether this attribute is inherited from the Angwins or from some other line is not known.

In 1658 a document[16] was signed by 155 men of St.Just engaging 'to be true and faithful to his Highness the Lord Protector' but Richard's signature does not appear although that of Malachay Angwin, a cousin, does. A Thomas Guy and Isacke Penberthye were also signatories and it seems likely that these were the same people named in Richard's will as his nephew and kinsman respectively.

Richard, a man of substance, derived his wealth/income from land and tin interests. At his death in 1675 the total of his inventory was £227 but this amount did not include the value of his freehold land only a chattel estate worth £60. The inventory shows £20 for tin bounds but this sum too, may well not represent the total value of his tin interests. Nor does the inventory total include monies indicated in his will as owing to Richard.

It would appear that his brother-in-law Christopher Millett of St.Hilary, husband of his sister Honor, was the one most indebted to him as he was remitted and forgiven 'all such debts as is owing to me by Bond Bill or otherwise'. His godson Thomas Fleming was given a debt of £4 which was due from Thomas Fleminge, deceased, Richard's brother-in-law. His wife, Grace was given debts of £3 from the executors of the same Thomas Fleming,gent., deceased, £5 due from Thomas Sise of St.Ives, another £5 due from the executors of Nicholas Fleming, gent., deceased, late of Bone in Madron and 30 shillings due from Thomas Cowlinge, gent., together with the "benefit and profite" on them. In the event of nonpayment, his executor, Emanuel Millett was, in his name, to allow Grace "to sue and impleade" any defaulters.

Richard would also have had some cash but although he bequeathed various sums of money in his will the actual amount is not known. He left 10 shillings to the parson who preached his funeral sermon, £5 towards the repair of St.Just church (Plate 6b) and another £5 to the 'impotent' poor of that parish. Other bequests were personal. Thomas, Anne and Thomasine, the children of his cousin Bennett Angwin, deceased, were to have 3s 4d each. All his godchildren were bequeathed 5s except Josyas who was left 20s. As Josyas was both godson and one of Bennett's children this may be why he was left more than the other godchildren although, as his legacy totalled more than the godchildren's 5s plus the 3s 4d left to Bennett's children, he may have been somewhat a favourite. Monetary amounts from 5s to 20s were bequeathed to other people including family members and his household servants with the only large sum, £80, being left to his nephew Thomas Guy.

An assignment dated 1642,[17] indicates that as early as 1610 Richard was granted a lease on part of Bojewyan by Henry Angwin, his uncle. Other documents show he not only leased land but bought it, sometimes he purchased the land he was already leasing, spending something over £650 on parts of Bojewyan, Chyrose, and Keigwin. These parts varied in size from reasonably large portions down to just ¾ or ½ an acre, being 4 and 2 stitches respectively. Richard also inherited his father's holdings in Bojewyan and Chyrose.

He bought, for £170, from Joseph Gubbs, a Penzance merchant, part of Bosaverne which was sold by auction at St. Just Churchtown on 12 April 1664, with Richard opening the bidding at £100. A survey records the bids and bidders[18]:
Richard Angwin £100, £125, £135, £140, £150, £160, £170;
Peter Casley who, with Justinian Edwards, was in possession of the land, £110, £130, £165;
Paskow Sanders £120.

Although Richard continued the Angwin family's long involvement with tin it is not clear how or when his interests were acquired. All that is known is that included in his purchase of part of Chyrose in 1660[19] were not only grist mills but also stamping mills and crazing mills.

His father Martin left his land to Richard. To his other son, also called Martin, he left his tin interests being half of the middle stamps, the buddle place, a third of the bounds and a way to carry the tin, at an unspecified location, but probably at Chyrose. In return for Richard having nothing to do with these tin interests, Martin had to hand over to Richard the lands his father had previously passed to him. Martin was buried in 1668 and presumably it was his will that was proved at Exeter in that year. Unfortunately it was one of the ones destroyed by enemy action in 1942 so it is not known what he left or to whom. He does not appear to have had issue so it is likely that Richard inherited much, if not all, his brothers assets including his tin interests.

In his will Richard left a fourth part of the Tinbounds in Cornwall 'solely possessed' by him together with a fourth part, with profits, of all other 'Tinbounds wherein' he was 'concerned with other men' to his nephew Thomas Guy. Another nephew, Martin Millett, was also left a fourth part of all his solely possessed tin bounds. His kinsman, Isacke Penberthye, was to have the fourth part of Richard's rights and interest in pairs of bounds at Wheale Reath in Buswarthen Downs in Sancreed parish and three others called Burtenye, Carneglase and Croft and Dergh in St. Just parish. The remainder of his bounds went to his nephew and sole executor, Emanuel Millett, who also inherited Richard's estates in Bojewyan and Chyrose including the mills.

Although their uncle was an astute business man his nephews, Emanuel Millett and Thomas Guy, do not appear to have had the same business acumen. In the years immediately following Richard's death they not only mortgaged and sold their inheritance but also got into debt.[20] For instance, in 1679 Bosaverne, which had been inherited by Thomas Guy, was acquired by John Borlase in discharge of a debt of £136 14s due from Thomas made up of an outstanding mortgage with interest, £53 for white tin, £79 10s and £4 4s for money lent to him at various times.[21]

William Scawen, a vice warden of the Stannaries, writing on the decay of Cornish, records that Richard's relations had suits before him for tin bounds. Wanting to preserve what he could of the Cornish language he had, perhaps hoping to turn this situation to his advantage, extracted a promise from them of being given a manuscript that Richard had translated from Cornish into English. Unfortunately before Richard's relations returned home "their people tearing all about for their controverted goods had torn into pieces all these papers".[22]

Perhaps it was because his executor was not such a good business man as himself that Richard appointed his 'kind friends Mr. Hugh Pawley and Mr. James Millett my overseers, whome I desire to use their best endeavors to see my will performed and to quiett and appease all differences if any shall happen betweene my executor and the legatees before named'. In particular he may have thought that Emanuel would not be able to pay the sum of £80 bequeathed to Thomas Guy. If he could not, it was to be lawful for Thomas to enter certain of Emanuel's fields in Bojewyan "to hold posses and quietly enjoy" until he received his money, but as the money was paid over this did not happen.

While from Martin's inventory the household goods inherited by Richard can be seen in detail they cannot, unfortunately, be compared with those that Richard had at the time of his death as these were not detailed. Even though a few were mentioned in his will no real comparison can be made to see if the house was more comfortably or more luxuriously furnished at that time. As the total value of the goods in the main rooms had increased only by a pound or two it would suggest that the furnishings were much the same.

The household goods listed in Martin's inventory were much as one would expect for a gentleman of his status. He had the usual items of furniture and kitchen ware, including a skillet, a pair of andirons, 3 iron spits, 2 brandises, together with napry, pewter, a pepper corn mill and seven silver spoons. Richard's inventory also mentions silver spoons but only five although, according to his will, he also had a silver bowl.

PEPPERMILL

It is interesting to note an apparent change in farming practice between Richard and his father. Martin was a sheep farmer as, except for 2 kind left to his wife in his will, the only stock mentioned in his inventory were 24 sheep, 6 lambs and swine. Richard however, as well as having 21 sheep, 9 lambs and pigs, had a bull, 3 steers, 2 yearlings, 4 heifers, 10 cows, goats and kids. Both grew corn. Martin had an ox and Richard 4 oxen to work the land. The former also had a nag and a mare, the latter 3 nags, 4 mares and a colt. Both kept poultry.

It is not easy to know with whom Richard mixed socially. He was obviously in close contact with various members of his family and in his will recorded Mr. Hugh Pawley and Mr. James Millet, who became vicar of St. Just in 1678, as his friends. Other friends must surely, have included Amos Mason, the then vicar of St. Just, Robert Colman and John Busvargus the witnesses to his will. His inventory does not hint at further friends or associates as the appraisers Christopher Millett and Malachais Angwin were relatives. He would also have known, if not been friends with, members of families of similar status to himself such as the Lanyons, Borlases and the Usticks all of whom were near neighbours.

Richard's widow, Grace was buried at Madron in 1678. Although Richard had no children to carry on his line other branches of the family thrived, some staying in St. Just parish even until today. Others spread out into West Penwith and further afield, with, like so many Cornish in the 1800s, many emigrating to places overseas, particularly Australia where numerous of their descendants are still to be found.

References
1. Edited by P.A.S.Pool in JRIC New Series Vol.III, part 3, 1959.
2. Senar was the old form of Zennor & according to Pool Innyal was apparantly the old name for Gurnard's Head where the only chapel, Chapel Jane, was on Zennor cliffs.
3. RIC Henderson Collection - Documents relating to Angwin lands 1560-1699
4. Vivian's Visitations
5. RIC HM4/11
6. RIC HM4/39
7. CRO HM4/41, will Richard Angwin 1675, original, CRO, copy, RIC
8. CRO A225/1
9. Vivian's Visitations
10. CRO A225/2
11. CRO Inventory Richard Angwin 1675
12. RIC, CRO, will Richard Angwin 1675
13. JRIC 1930 part 2 p327
14. RIC HM4/41
15. Memorials of John Ray 1846 p189-90
16. St Just A Statistical Account by Rev John Buller Pub.1842 & facsimile 1983
17. RIC HM4/11
18. RIC HHJ2/24
19. RIC HM4/29
20. RIC Henderson Collection - of various documents
21. RIC HHJ2/39
22. The Parochial History of Cornwall by Davies Gilbert Vol.4 p218

X THE QUAKERS AT SENNEN

GILLIAN GREEN

Why do we feel a pang of regret, and pay silent homage as we go past the old Quaker cemetery (Plate 7a and b) at Treave on the border of Sennen Parish.[10] Neglected and overgrown with brambles it unfailingly claims our attention. In the past, great men have suffered for their faith, but the 35 - 40 Quakers buried there 300 years ago, were simple-hearted, honest people, fishermen, shepherds, weavers, farmers and small traders. They were called upon to endure imprisonment, banishment, fines, robbings, beatings and spittings from their so-called fellow Christians.

In 1646 George Fox founded the `Quakers' or `Society of Friends' in northern England, after he had a profound religious experience[1]. At a time of great internal strife in the Church of England, he preached that there was no need for ministers, liturgy, sacrament, music or sanctuary. Man could follow his own inner spirit, guided by his conscience. He rejected war and violence, as well as swearing of oaths and paying of tithes to the Church. In silence they would worship, in the presence of God, and only speaking when moved. They believed in the good things of life - a relaxed and loving home, a good table, unostentatious clothes of grey homespun and blue cloth. They did not withdraw from the framework of society. They believed in work, steady days of labour, honestly performed. Equality for women was important to them and they were permitted to preach, but this was not favoured by the Cornish. They used no titles - just Christian names.

George Fox travelled extensively and in 1655[2] he arrived in 'The Dark Country' of Cornwall. It was his custom to ask at the inn for names of the 'honest and good' but in Royalist Cornwall it was more difficult to find these people than in the Parliamentary north. Inn keepers deliberately kept names from him, but there were little groups of followers at Truro, Breage, Helston, Marazion and Sennen.

He wrote a paper for the seven parishes of Land's End and distributed them. Whilst in St. Ives he was arrested with Edward Pyott and William Salt by Justice Seeley. The interested townspeople were in uproar. Accompanied by a guard of soldiers under Captain John Keate, they were taken in calculated cruelty the 50 miles to Launceston Castle, and thrown into a roofless chamber twelve feet square. Here for nine weeks they languished, awaiting the March Assizes under Sir John Glyn, Chief Justice of England. They refused to remove their hats as a mark of respect, and refused to pay his suggested fines. Re-imprisoned in an underground cell called Doomsdale, they were fed by free Quakers. They appealed to Oliver Cromwell, who sent his personal chaplain, a Cornishman called Hugh Peters, to visit Launceston and Pendennis Castles. Peters told his master "They can't do Fox a greater service than to imprison him in Cornwall". Peters knew the generous hearts of his fellow Cornishmen and their hatred of injustice.

William Penn said of Fox,[3] "Above all, he excelled in prayer - the inwardness and weight of spirit, the reverence and solemnity of his address and behaviour struck even strangers with admiration". Major General Desbrough offered freedom if they would go straight home and preach no more. After nine months they were released and Fox rode to Tregangeeves in St. Tudy, a great Quaker stronghold, and the home of Loveday Hamblyn.

In 1663 Fox was back in Sennen at Brea, the home of John Ellis, a Royalist Cavalier, landowner and ardent Quaker. The local group of Friends met secretly in Brea Farmhouse. Despite being separated from the other groups by bad roads and long distances, small groups met once in 1658, quarterly in 1660 and monthly from 1666 to '69. Travelling Quakers carried newsletters from group to group.

John Ellis gave part of his land for the burial site, which was surrounded by a high 10 feet wall. It was 54 feet long and 46 feet broad, with flat ground inside. Two upright stones on the St. Just roadside suggest an old opening. Quaker graveyards were always small and some had meeting houses inside. There could have been one in this graveyard as records show a meeting house at Treave. Present day farmers have no recollection of any meeting houses on their land but the field north of and adjacent to the burial ground is called Burial Ground Field. Local folklore claims sightings, on many occasions, of a horseman followed by a dog leaping the wall in the adjacent field. This might be the staunch John Ellis. The first burial in 1659 was Barbara, his two year old daughter. John Ellis's wife Phillipa was buried in 1677 and her massive granite tombstone (Plate 7b) is the only visible grave today.

When Charles II came to the throne in 1660 he promised the Quakers liberty of conscience, and that none should wrong or abuse them. A year later he broke his word at the rise of the Fifth Monarchy Men.[4] By the Quaker Act of 1662 no one of any sect was allowed to hold religious meetings of more than five people.

Charles Henderson, the noted young Cornish historian, records in a newspaper article[5] that confiscations were in the form of livestock, household utensils (mostly pewter), farm products, money, shop goods, tools, clothing, bedding, saddlery, furniture and tobacco. The seizers kept the goods, or they were sold cheaply by the judges.

SOME NOTES FROM CORNISH RECORDS[6,7]:

JOHN ELLIS.
1657 John Ellis summoned to appear before Peter Seeley for not raising his hat to Peter Seeley and James Launce in Penzance. Thrown into Doomsdale, Launceston Gaol and cruelly used by jailers.

Taken from John Ellis one horse, by suit of Thomas Quarum and Richard Whiteforde who farmed the tithe of the Priest of Sennen.

Had taken from him by Degory Wallish and Ralfe Jeffry, churchwardens, three pewter platters and one pewter pegger worth twelve shillings for a six shilling rate towards the repair of the steeplehouse.

Also taken from him by Thomas Trereefe and Martin Williams a pewter platter worth 6s for rate of 2s.6d. Thomas Trereefe returned it again as he only took it when threatened by Peter Seeley. His conscience would not allow him to keep it.

John Ellis went to Marazion Market where Peter Seeley accosted him with false accusations and questioned him why he dared to travel five miles from his home. Seeley and the Mayor of Marazion sent him to Launceston Gaol, and after imprisonment of three sessions released him as they found no charge against him.

1658 23rd August, John Ellis was served with a special warrant at the instigation of Pascoe Tresilian who farmed the tithe of Joseph Hull, Priest of Sennen, for failure to pay the tithes. Nicholas Dever and another bailiff took his cloak and spurs and placed him on a saddleless horse to take him to Launceston Gaol. A relative witnessed this planned cruelty and paid the tithes for him.

John Ellis had a debt of 9s detained from him by Edmond Nicholas who asserted that Ellis owed 5s.4d towards repairs of the Steeple house. He kept the 9s which he owed Ellis for pasturing some of his young bullocks.

1659 Thomas Quarme who farmed the tithe of the priest of Sennen got an execution out of the Hundred Court of Penwith against the body of John Ellis and caused him to be arrested by four bailiffs who carried him to James Christopher's house, being head bailiff of the hundred, and put in a room eleven feet long and seven feet broad, with many other prisoners, which place became very nasty and stinking and one of them was like to have died. The wickedness of the aforesaid keeper was more towards John Ellis than the other prisoners. He would not open the door for Mrs. Ellis to pass food to her husband and she was forced to feed him through a tiny hole in the door. She secreted small flasks of water into him.

1660 Sued in the Hundred Court of Penwith by Pasco Tresilian, farmer of Priest Hull's tithe. Passing through Penzance, arrested by the sergeant of Penzance and thrown in the mire and searched for arms and imprisoned.

1670 Taken off John Ellis for a meeting held in his house - one mare and colt valued at £1.10s.0d.

Taken from Dorothy Ellis daughter of John Ellis by the officers of Sennen Parish for being present at The Meeting - one colt and one rearing calf value £1.10s.0d.

Taken from Elizabeth and Phillippa Ellis, two other daughters, for being at The Meeting - two rearing calves worth £1.8s.0d.

NICHOLAS JOSE
1657 Nicholas Jose is well remembered as a Quaker preacher and was a fisherman/farmer with a shop. A field at Treave is still called Shop Field. He married Ebezat of Senninge. They had a son Nicholas, born 1666, and three daughters, Rebecka, Mary and Honour. In 1642 Nicholas Jose signed the Protestation Return, and in The Tudor Muster Roll of 1569 this well-established family had three males who were prominent in carrying arms.

1657 Nicholas Jose at harvest time had taken from him by officers of the Priest Hull without the showing of a warrant, 39 sheaves of rye for tithes.

1658 Nicholas Jose again at harvest time had taken by the servant of Pasco Tresilian who farmed the priest's tithe, without a warrant, 33 sheaves of rye.

For refusing to pay 6d towards repairs of steeplehouse taken from Nicholas Jose one pewter platter worth 3s.8d, by Edmonde Nicholas and John Richards.

As Nicholas Jose was traveling upon the highway one Thomas Treave the elder, of the parish of Sennen attacked him with ropes and stones and spilt his blood. Michael Richards and John Saundry the constables were informed, but did nothing to punish Treave.

1660   On passing through Truro Nicholas Jose was taken by armed guards before John Chaty, the mayor, and he refused to take the Oath of Allegiance. He was kept a week in the town gaol and then taken to Launceston Gaol for five months.

1661   Nicholas Jose with Friends at Mabe was caught worshipping The Lord. Fifty musketeers with swords drawn burst in and were very rude and uncivil. All taken to Pendennis Castle and cast into a dark dungeon. Then to Penryn town hall and on to Truro. John Polwheele and Degory Polwheele, justices, asked them to take the Oath of Allegiance, but for conscience sake they could not swear and went on to Launceston Gaol where they remained five months.

1662   Nicholas Jose again caught in St. Just with Friends when Captain Jones and soldiers burst in and arrested all the company. Taken before William Godolphin who sent them to Launceston Gaol. The four ringleaders including Jose imprisoned 5½ years and the remainder for 2 years.

A QUAKER LADY

1670   Officers of the parish of Sennen fine Nicholas Jose one brass pan and one chair worth £1 for a fine of 5s imposed on his wife for being at a meeting while Jose was in prison.

1677   Prosecuted by Hugh Jones in the Hundred Court. George Treweege the hundred bailiff took goods worth £1.4s.6d at one time and at another time took goods to the value of £14.8s.0d. Later Jones sent his servant to the shop of Jose and took and carried away goods worth upwards of £10 - all taken for a tithe of 1½ acres. Hugh Jones repeatedly sent his clerk each harvest time to take sheaves of corn - as much as he could carry.

1682   Jose was praemunired (meaning 'out of the King's protection') lands and goods forfeited to the King and remained a prisoner at the King's pleasure until 1685.

GEORGE READ

1658   George Read was a member of another prominent Quaker family at Sennen. For refusing to pay 6d for repairs to Steeplehouse he had taken by Edmund Nicholas and John Richards - one pewter platter worth 3s.8d.

1660   George Read caught at St. Just Meeting of Friends with George John, Tobyas Read, and John Tonckyn. They were taken to Truro before Justice Walter Vincent and John Vivian and sent to Launceston Gaol for eight weeks.

1661   Hugh Jones of the parish Sennen who farmed the tithe of Priest Hull took from George Read one fat oxen worth £4 and one mare worth £5.

1662   George Read and John Stevens of Botreaux Castle brought from their labours by guards to William Cotton, justice, who tended the Oath of Allegiance and sent them to Launceston Gaol for refusing to take it. Imprisoned 13 weeks.

1670   Taken from George Read by John Mathew and Nicholas Wallish, constables and John Trereeve and Thomas Trereeve wardens by a warrant from Hugh Jones, justice, for permitting a Meeting of Friends at his home and being present - three milch cows and one horse valued at £12.

JOHN MATHEWS

1661   John Mathews had two hearths in the Hearth Tax. For conscience sake he could not bear arms in the 'trained band' (17th Century equivalent of a Defence Militia) and was sent to Launceston Gaol for 10 days by William Godolphin and William Pendarvis, justices.

1662   Arrested at house of Nicholas Jose by Captain Jones and soldiers. William Godolphin sent them to gaol at Launceston for two years as no surety of good behaviour.

1683   John Mathews, Isaac Chappell, John Tonckyn and Richard Richards, Jone Olivy and Wilmott Richards sent by Hugh Jones, justice, for attending a meeting to Launceston Gaol. They came before the infamous Judge Jeffryes of 'The Bloody Assizes' [8]. After very careful consideration and already primed by the great Quaker Thomas Lower, he discharged the prisoners much to the grief and vexation of Justice Hugh Jones.

1684   Again Justice Hugh Jones imprisoned John Mathew, Richard Richards, Jenkin Vingoe, John Tonckyn, and Sampson Olivey for unlawful assembly in Sennen. Judge Mountague set them all free.

In 1685 there was a pardon for the Quakers, who by passive resistance had won their reward. By 1738 there were 38 regular Quaker Societies in Cornwall. After 1750 there was a certain decline as Methodism took over the County.

I shall let W.C. Braithwaite[9] have the final word:

> "A spiritual dignity enabled the Quaker to be himself, without pretence, in any company, with warm domestic affection, little softness, and no frivolity – art and learning were not important to him, lives were occupied with faithful discharge of responsibilities, crowned with the happiness of work worthily done, fierce in the witness of truth, but tender in love to man, tested and purified in the fires of suffering and self-sacrifice yet not without the consolations of inward spiritual joy."

References
1. Conversations with Mrs. P.M. Griffith, Archivist for The Quakers of Cornwall today.
2. Cornish Riviera, by J. Harris Stone. 1912.
3. William Penn. Great Quaker who founded Pennsylvania in America. 1644-1718.
4. Nutthall Encyclopedia. 1990. Ed. by Rev. James Wood.
5. Charles Henderson. Historian of Cornwall. Newspaper article in Western Morning News, 5th July, 1928. .R.I.C. Records.
6. The Record of Sufferings of Friends in Cornwall, 1655 to 1792. 1655 to 1686 by Dr. Thomas Lower, step son-in-law to George Fox. Transcribed by Norman Penney, 1928.
7. Penwith Local History Index Cards of the Parishes in Penwith in 16th and 17th Centuries from Parish Records of Births, Deaths and Marriages.
8. Judge Jeffreys 1648-89. Famous for 'The Bloody Assizes' in Monmouth Rebellion.
9. William C. Braithwaite Ll.B 'The Penal Laws affecting Early Friends in England.
10. J. Harris Stone. Reprint of 'Gasgoine Map of 1696" by Exeter University. 1922.

XI FRANCIS PAYNTER AND HIS FAMILY IN THE LATE 1600s

J. M. HOSKING

St. Buryan parish has been the cradle of several families who became famous. The Levelis family left Trewoofe in mid 1600s after more than 400 years of occupation, due to the lack of a male heir. The Pender family of Pendrea too, had gone by the late 1600s. Those Penders of Trevider were soon to go to Penryn. The Noye family had produced William Noye, High Treasurer to Charles I, and were by this time in decline. They sold the Manor of St. Buryan in 1680.

The Boscawen family of Boscawen-rose had long since gone to Tregothnan, married wealth and achieved fame in the form of Admiral Boscawen. Likewise, the Vyvyan family had long since moved from Trevedran to Trelowarren and respectability after feuding, abductions and a few murders! About this time too the Grose family left Rosmodress, whilst the Ustickes of Leah stayed on for another 100 years.

However, it is to Francis Paynter that I would draw your attention - born at Trelissick, St. Erth in 1639, a younger son of William Paynter and Jane Keigwin of Mousehole. His brother William became Rector of Exeter College, Oxford, and Vice-Chancellor of Oxford University. His elder brother, Arthur, married Mary Praed and lived at Trelissick, the family home.

William Paynter, the elder, bought Boskenna, St. Buryan, for his son Francis in the late 1670s. The property was purchased on a mortgage from a cousin, Admiral Carthew. A Walter Carthew had bought Boskenna almost 100 years before this. Because the Admiral had gambled all his money away, Francis Paynter allowed him to remain at Boskenna, living in one room with his two dogs. He became the huntsman in charge of the local pack of hounds of which he had previously been the owner.

In 1676, Francis Paynter bought Lower Boskennal, St. Buryan, from a Mr. Tippett and also purchased Higher Boskennal on a 99 year Lease and there he lived whilst improvements were being made at Boskenna. In later years he returned to this property and was known as Francis Paynter of Boskennal.

In Lake's Parochial History of Cornwall,[1] it is recorded that "Mr. Francis Paynter by his skill and husbandry...and some helps of the law, has purchased to himself a very fair younger brother's inheritance. Though this place (Boskenna) lies near the sea and very much exposed, yet has this gentleman by means of furze ricks and other ingenious contrivances raised several fair walks of trees about it, and made it a pleasant seat." To add to his comfort Francis had brought with him from Trelissick a great Jacobean bed. In 1671 Francis signed a legal letter written at Boskenna and from 1672 the parish registers for St. Buryan record baptisms for children of the family. However, members of the Paynter family consider they owned the land from 1676.

JACOBEAN BED- CARVED AND CURTAINED

Francis married twice. There were children by his first wife and one son James, survived. Francis's second wife was Margaret Paulett, whom he married in about 1670. She was the daughter of Sir Henry Paulett of Kilburn Priory, Middlesex. She brought considerable property with her. Wealthy though she was, she allowed the servants only half an egg each for breakfast. The arms of Paynter impaled with Paulett are built into a gable at Boskenna with the date '1678' carved in granite. The house was rebuilt during this time and the farmhouse also adjoined it.

According to Tonkin,[1] Mr. Francis Paynter "Was formerly one of the clerks of the Admiralty and is now General Receiver of Prize Money which shall become due to captors". In the St. Buryan parish registers, it is recorded that the Dean of St. Buryan leased tithes for three years to Hugh Jones, Esq. of Penrose and to Francis Paynter of Boskenna amounting to £240 at 30th March, 1683.

Francis Paynter acquired wealth in various ways and not always honourably it would seem, sometimes in collusion with his brother Arthur of Trelissick. In 1665 one of Francis Paynter's cousins, a William Paynter of Tremearne, Germoe, had debts, some of which Francis Paynter paid off for him. There were other debts and William assigned the rents and profits on two-thirds of Tremearne to Francis, who in return went bail for him.

Later, William sold lands (which were already mortgaged to Francis) to a Christopher Cork. Francis seized possession of those lands in 1680 and "kept more than his legal entitlement", so William said in court in 1681. Francis promised to secure William's release from Bodmin jail if he signed certain deeds over to him. This William did without reading them first hoping to be freed, but it is said, Francis left him in prison. When William was eventually set free his cousin Thomas Hawkins had him arrested again for a small debt. He was kept at the Bailiff's House for a few days, then taken to Francis Paynter's house at St. Buryan. There Francis forced him to sign over property to him.

Conversely, Francis was considered a religious man. Books on Divinity were to be found in his library. His eminent brother, William Paynter D.D. (earlier referred to) became rector of Wootten, Northamptonshire. His own son, Thomas, was curate of Sennen and St. Levan, later vicar of Sithney. Francis had obvious church connections.

By 1693 Francis had become Town Clerk of Penzance. Various references to him are recorded by the late Peter Pool in his 'History of Penzance',[2] more especially in connection with the dispute between John Carveth and Thomas Rowe, Vicar of Madron. Carveth had served two terms as mayor.

After a disputed election there were two mayors of Penzance. Carveth attempted to appoint a new curate of St. Mary's Chapel without reference to the Vicar of Madron. The Vicar acted firmly, supported by the bishop, Sir Jonathan Trelawny. Francis Paynter took a letter to the bishop who was at that time in London. Carveth was forced to abandon both claims. Francis Paynter was appointed as one of the commissioners to swear in the new mayor.

No doubt an interesting meeting took place between Bishop Trelawney and Paynter. The bishop was Dean of St. Buryan as well as Bishop of Exeter. (Bishop Trelawney, one of the six Bishops who had been imprisoned in the Tower, was an ancestor of the late Diana Princess of Wales)

The Paynters were ardent Royalists and had melted down the family plate for the cause. In the house over the mantelpiece for many years hung an oil painting of James II. Beside it were two little medallions of Charles I and his queen Henrietta Maria, together with a chair that Charles I had sat on, which were among prized possessions. Another historical memento was a book with silver clasps, containing a manuscript list of all the ships in the Navy in 1701. Eventually, Francis moved back to Boskennal and his son Francis, took possession of Boskenna.

BOOK WITH TWO SILVER CLASPS

There was always a certain danger of isolated raids carried out from foreign vessels on those who lived near the shore. The story is told of what happened on 29th July 1711.[3] "A French privateer landed at St. Loy (Boskenna foreshore) robbed a house and afterwards went on shore (again) at Penberth, carried away two boats, some sheep and two men from the village and made them bring their women from on board ye boates. They made them (i.e. the women) compound for their freedom and after the penalty was paid, kept the men and kept the tackle and sent the women and the boats to the shore...This same Frenchman afterwards landed men and took some sheep at Porthgwarra"[3] These kinds of incidents would no doubt have made going out of the family home a hazard for well-brought up young ladies, and anyone else, who lived near the coast.

The second Francis and his brother James, had a sister Diana, young enough to be their daughter. Ustick writes in July, 1711[3], "Mr James Paynter is gone for Diana and Mr. Hawkins; the person she dined with at Burnewhall". It seems that Diana, aged seventeen, had gone off to her cousin's house and James was sent to bring her back. It was no time for allowing young ladies of seventeen too much liberty, however innocent the occasion. Even though it was not yet dark; dinner was an early meal and Burnewhall but a mile from Boskenna.

We have to look at the first Francis's life as being led in very harsh times and although many of his actions cannot be admired, he laid the foundations for the Paynter family at St. Buryan for many generations. Eight generations of the Paynter family lived at Boskenna over a period of two hundred and eighty years. Their stay is fascinating and their colourful lives are a part of St. Buryan history.

Paynter family seal

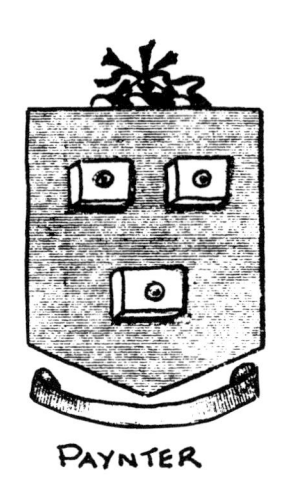

PAYNTER

Will of the First Francis Paynter of Boskenna and Boskennal

PAYNTER, FRANCIS of Boskennall in Buryan, by his will 13 June 1723, proved in the Peculiar court of the Deanery of Burian chapel Royal 1 Aug. 1724, gave to his wife Margaret Paynter, the tenements called Boskennall, which he purchased from Mr. Tippett, to hold during her life, also the tenements which he held by leases from rt. hon. Hugh Boscawen and John Trevanion to hold during her life, also the messuages called Galligan in Burian, and all the messuages and houses in Burian church town which he held by lease, during her life, and as long as she lives at Boskennal the use of all the furniture, etc. To his dear friend and son in law Francis Paynter of Trelissick, his son Francis Paynter of Boskenna, and his friends William Gwavas of Penzance, and George Veale of Trevailer, all his lands, &c. in Wilsdon and Acton in Middlesex upon trust. All his chattell leases, lands &c. called Rosemodres, Roselucomb, the Gawes, the Ninnicks and the Tregiffiens all in Burian, to them in trust, to sell, pay debts and equally divide to all his children living (except to his eldest son Francis Paynter on whom he settled an estate in his lifetime). All his other lands in Burian, Breag, Marazion, etc., which he settled on his son Francis on his marriage, if his heirs fail, then to his son Thomas Paynter, then in default to his son Arthur Paynter and so on to other sons; Overplus of sale to his daughter Mary, wife of Thomas Haweis of Chincoose, gent., her share to remain till T. Haweis settle a jointure of some estate on his wife. To the indigent of S. Berian £4, To the indigent of Sennen, St. Levan and St. Erth £2 each. In witness my hand and seal 13 June 1723. Hear I take of my seal and declare this to be my last will and testament, Fran. Paynter. Witnesses Mary Paynter, Stephen Bodinar and Francis Carne.

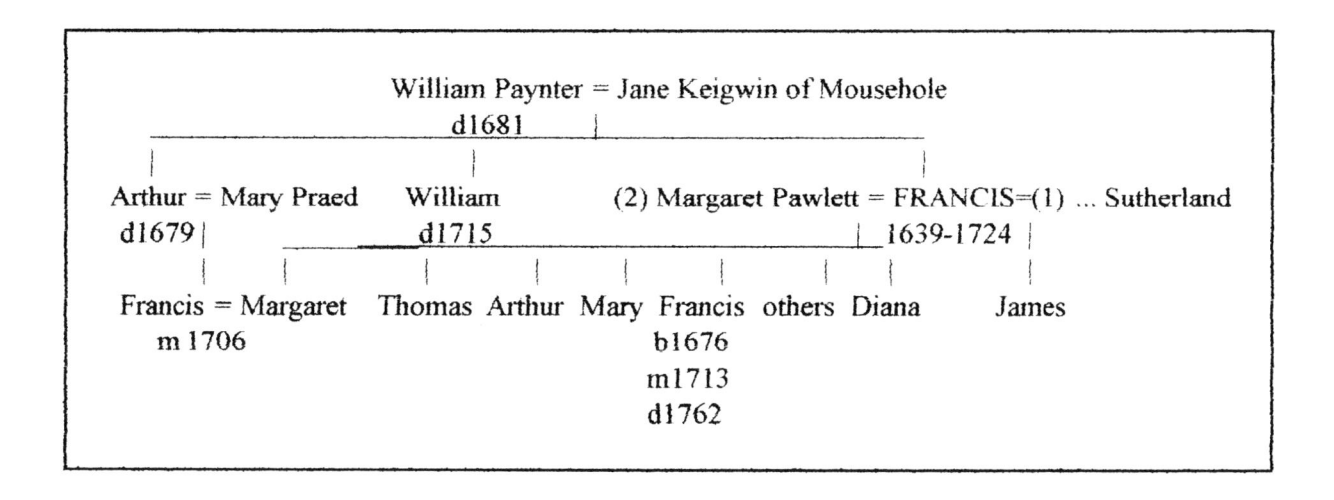

```
                    William Paynter = Jane Keigwin of Mousehole
                         d1681
   |                    |                         |
Arthur = Mary Praed   William        (2) Margaret Pawlett = FRANCIS=(1) ... Sutherland
d1679|                 d1715                              | 1639-1724  |
   |         |          |      |      |      |      |       |             |
Francis = Margaret  Thomas Arthur Mary Francis others Diana              James
   m 1706                              b1676
                                       m1713
                                       d1762
```

References and acknowledgements
1. Thomas Tonkin as quoted in Lake's Parochial History of Cornwall
   and in The Parochial History of Cornwall Ed. Davis Gilbert 1838
2. History of the Town and Borough of Penzance, P.A.S. Pool 1974
3. MS Diary of Usticke of Nancealverne in the Morrab Library, Penzance.

My thanks to Mary Paynter née Haweis, wife of Reginald Paynter, for use of her notes.
I have quoted from leases and wills at the CRO and leases of Boskennal in my possession, and from Mr. Tom Paynter's book   on the The Paynter family in the RIC.

This article is part of a book to be published shortly on the story of Boskenna and the Paynters.

GATHERING POOKS OF HAY ONTO A SLEDGE

SURNAMES INDEX

ADAMS 24,25
ANDREW 56
ANGWIN 59,60 61,62,63
ARUNDELL 55,57

BARAGWANATH 56,58
BEARD 54
BENMER 52,53,54
BENNET 8,9,60
BERRIMAN 29,58
BERRYMAN 27,30, 31,32,33
BLUNT 54
BODINAR 72
BORLASE 18,21,33 62,63
BOSCAWEN 69
BOSON 60
BOSUSTOW 11
BROWN 58
BUSVARGUS 63

CARA 1,14,15
CAREW 35,37
CARTHEW 69
CARVETH 70
CASLEY 61
CHAPPELL 68
CHATY 67
CHEKEMBRA 31
CHINVER 25
CHRISTOPHER 66
CLEVERDON 52,54
COCK 60
COCKIN 57
COELL 36,38
COLMAN 63
CORK 70
COTTON 68
COWLINGE 61
CROMWELL 64
CURNOW 55,58

DANIEL 49,50, 51,54
DAVYES 18
DENNIS 1
DESBROUGH 64
DEVER 66
DONITHORNE 8,25,32
DONN 8
DOWING 24,25
DOWINGE 8

EDDY 27,29,32, 33
EDWARDS 61
ELLIS 11,23,24,47,65,66
EVA 8,9

FOWLER 27,31
FOSSE 8

GENDALL 14
GEORGE 13,14,15
GINVER 24
GLYNN 64
GODOLPHIN 67,68
GRENVILLE 57
GROSE 8,69
GUBBS 49,50,52,53,54,61
GUY 61,62
GWAVAS 72
GWENNAP 54
GYLES 56

HALLAMORE 52
HAMBLYN 65
HARFORD 8
HARRIS 8
HARRY 49,50,54
HARVYE 12,14,15
HAWKINGE 56
HAWKYNS 70
HENDERSON 65
HICK 17,55
HINSON 8,9
HODGE 14,55,56,57
HOSKING 58
HULL 66
HUTCHINS 9

JAMES 8
JEFFERY 58
JEFFRYE 65
JEFFRYS 68
JENKEN 54
JENKYN 53
JOHN 8,27,32,33,67
JONES 11,67,68,70
JOSE 66,67,68

KEATE 64
KEIGWIN 50,60,69
KNIGHT 31

LADNER 25
LANYON 59,63
LAWEIS 72
LAWRENCE 36
LEVELIS 69
LOWER 68

MADDERN 27,29,30,33,54
MARTEN 8,25
MASON 63
MATHEW 68
MI(T)CHELL 14,15, 27,31,38,39,56,58
MILLETT 19,20,61,62,63
MOUNTAGUE 68
MOYLE 40

NEWMAN 8
NICHOLAS 12,14,66,67
NOTTELL 56
NOYE 69

ODGER 56
OLIVER 19
OLIV(E)Y 25,68
OSBORN(E) 58

PAINTER 25
PALMER 40
PAUL 57
PAULETT 70
PAWLEY 62,63
PAYNTER 55,69,70,71,72
PENBERTHY 61,62
PENDARVES 18,68
PENDER 69
PENN 64
PENROSE 49
PERRY 27,30,33,38
PETERS 64
PHILLIP 27,30,33
PHILLIPES 56
POLWHEELE 67
PORTHMEAR 27,31,33
PRAED 33,69
PYOTT 64

QUARME 66
QUARUM 65
QUICK 8,27,31,32,33,34, 55,56,57,58

RAY 60
READ 67,68
RENODEN 56,57,58
RENOWDEN 31
RICHARDS 12,14,15,67,68
ROBART 27,33
ROBERTS 27,30,31
ROGERS 53
RONDELL 19,31
ROSEMENEWES 55
ROSWALL 55,56,57
ROWE 70
RUSSELL 25,56

ST.AUBYN 6	THIERRY 6	UDY 27,29,31,33
	THOMAS 24,25,27,29,31,	UPCOTT 27,32
SALT 64	33,37,38,58	USTICKE 49,50,63,69,71
SANDERS 61	TIPPETT 69	
SAUNDRY 9,67	TON(C)KYN 55,67,68	VEALE 6,8,9,10,22
SCAWEN 62	TRAVEILOR 8	24,32,33
SCHELLINKS 4,6,9,10	TREAVE 67	VINGOE 68
SEELEY 64,65,66	TREGURTHA 27,32,33	VISICKE 8
SHEARME 52,54	TREGURTHEN 56	VYVIAN 69
SISE 61	TRELAWNY 71	
SKINNER 25	TREMENHEERE 52,53,54	WADGE 56,58
SMITH 18	TREREEFE 66,68	WALLIS 8
SMYTHE 18	TRESILLIAN 11,66	WALLISH 12,14,15,65,68
SOMERS 13,14,15	TREVANION 72	WARREN 9
STEVENS 27,32,33,	TREVEATHEN 54	WHITEFORDE 65
56,57,68	TREWEEGE 67	WILLIAMS 12,14,31,66
SWEETE 27,31,33	TREWHELLA 56,58	WOOLCOCK 58
	TRIPCONY 24,25	WORTH 52
	TRUTHWALL 29	
	TYAG 54	YOUNG 54

A DRUMMER

GLOSSARY

BED (BEAD): Usually referred to the mattress only.
CARPET: Thick fabric, commonly of wool, to cover tables, beds, etc. (but not floors).
CHAFING DISH. Held burning fuel for heating anything placed on it.
COOLE (COULE) : A large tub sometimes used for salting meat.
CUPBOARD: One or more shelves for holding cups, dishes, etc. It had no doors.
DOWLAS SHEETS: Made of coarse linen. (Daoulas or Doulas- S.E. of Brest, in Brittany).
DREPPINGE: Probably a container for dripping
FIELD BED (STEAD): An inferior bed or camp bed.
FLASKET: A folding basket held together by its handles.
FURNISHED: A bed furnished was a bed and its bedding.
KEEVE (KIEVE) : A large wooden vat.
KETTLE: A metal container for cooking food.
KILDERKIN: A cask of about 18 gallons
MAZER (MAZOR): A polished wood or metal bowl (illustration chapter V)
PEWTER PEGGER: Possibly a Peg Tankard- a drinking vessel having each individual's share marked off by a nob.
PODGER: or PORRINGER: Bowls for soup or porridge.
POSNET or SKILLET: Small metal cooking pot with a handle and three short feet.
SAUCER: Any circular small, shallow or deep plate.
SAVING IRON: Perhaps a save-all for saving candle-ends for re-use.
SCRUFF OF BRASS: Possibly a vessel coated with brass.
SLAYES (REEDS): Used by weavers. A narrow, movable wooden frame fitted with reed or metal strips to separate the warp threads. A `pair' refers to a slaye with a beater (batten) that is used to beat down the weft threads.
STANDARD: Perhaps a measuring vessel.
TASTER: A small implement for tasting food or wine.
TRUCKLER (TRUNDLE) BEDSTEAD: A low bed on wheels which could be kept under another (illustration Chapter IV)

MENDING BEFORE THE HEARTH - FURZE AND TURF LAID READY TO BURN.